CHAMBERS

GUIDE TO

ENGLISH FOR I.T. AND THE INTERNET

Lesley Gourlay

GW00702909

CHAMBERS

CHAMBERS
An imprint of Chambers Harrap Publishers Ltd
7 Hopetoun Crescent
Edinburgh
EH7 4AY

A CIP catalogue record for this book is available from the British Library.

ISBN 0550 14007 7

The British National Corpus is a collaborative initiative carried out by
Oxford University Press, Longman, Chambers Harrap, Oxford University
Computing Services, Lancaster University's Unit for Computer Research
in the English Language, and the British Library. The project received
funding from the UK department of Trade and Industry and the Science
and Engineering Research Council, and was supported by additional
research grants from the British Academy and the British Library.

Publishing Manager
Elaine Higgleton

Series Editor
Penny Hands

Typeset by Chambers Harrap Publishers Ltd
Printed and bound in Great Britain by
Clays Ltd, St Ives plc

Contents

A note on trademarks

Contributors

Written by
Lesley Gourlay

Publishing Manager
Elaine Higgleton

Senior Editor
Penny Hands

Technical Consultant
Chris Whincop

Introduction

Chambers Guide to English for I.T. and the Internet aims to help learners of English understand and use the language of this fascinating and fast-moving area.

For many people, the world of computing can seem complex and strange. Such feelings can increase for learners of English, faced with a set of specialized terms and expressions in another language. The aim of this book is to clarify this area of language use, so that learners may feel more confident about using English in computing.

The book is not intended for computer specialists, although they may find it useful. It has been compiled with normal users of computers in mind – people who perhaps have a home computer, use computers at work, or in education. For this reason, it does not attempt to include all the specialist terms used in computing, but concentrates on words and expressions which are likely to be useful to the general user. It is a language guide, not a computer manual.

Chambers Guide to English for I.T. and the Internet covers the following topics:

o the major areas in which computers are used

o common words and expressions, shown in clear, graded, explanatory text

o dialogues showing how common expressions are used by speakers in a variety of contexts

o language boxes highlighting how particular words or groups of words are used

o help with pronunciation of many terms

o special panels showing how different styles of speech or writing are used in different computing situations

o illustrations showing e-mails, screenshots and diagrams.

Computing is an ever-changing field, and new terms are constantly introduced and discarded as the technology develops and moves forward. Because of this, we have only included very recent terms if we consider that they are likely to stay in use long enough for them to be interesting to the general user.

The book begins by looking at the elements of a computing system, and moves on to look at programs, and what they are used for. A large part of the book is concerned with applications which are commonly used in everyday life. Finally, there are chapters on the Internet and the World Wide Web, and on e-mail.

American English spellings are often used in references to elements of particular kinds of software, as these are common in computing and the Internet.

The book is oriented towards PC users, although Mac users should still find the majority of the points relevant.

We hope that people with a wide range of backgrounds and interests – academic, personal or business – will enjoy using this book, and that it will encourage them in their ability to benefit from the global communication that has been made possible by such technology.

Pronunciation guide

Key to the phonetic symbols used in this book

CONSONANTS

p	/piː/	pea
t	/tiː/	tea
k	/kiː/	key
b	/biː/	bee
d	/daɪ/	dye
g	/gaɪ/	guy
m	/miː/	me
n	/njuː/	new
ŋ	/sɒŋ/	song
θ	/θɪn/	thin
ð	/ðɛn/	then
f	/fan/	fan
v	/van/	van
s	/siː/	sea
z	/zuːm/	zoom
ʃ	/ʃiː/	she
ʒ	/beɪʒ/	beige
tʃ	/iːtʃ/	each
dʒ	/ɛdʒ/	edge
h	/hat/	hat

VOWELS
Short vowels

ɪ	/bɪd/	bid
ɛ	/bɛd/	bed
a	/bad/	bad
ʌ	/bʌd/	bud
ɒ	/pɒt/	pot
ʊ	/pʊt/	put
ə	/əˈbaʊt/	about

Long vowels

iː	/biːd/	bead
ɑː	/hɑːm/	harm
ɔː	/ɔːl/	all
uː	/buːt/	boot
ɜː	/bɜːd/	bird

Diphthongs

eɪ	/beɪ/	bay
aɪ	/baɪ/	buy
ɔɪ	/bɔɪ/	boy
aʊ	/haʊ/	how

l	/leɪ/	lay	oʊ	/goʊ/	go
r	/reɪ/	ray	ɪə	/bɪə(r)/	beer
j	/jɛs/	yes	ɛə	/bɛə(r)/	bare
w	/weɪ/	way	ʊə	/pʊə(r)/	poor

Notes

(1) The stress mark (') is placed before the stressed syllable (eg. invent /ɪn'vɛnt/).

(2) The symbol (r) is used to represent *r* when it comes at the end of a word, to indicate that it is pronounced when followed by a vowel (as it is in 'four' in the phrase four or five /fɔːr ɔː 'faɪv/).

1

Computers and computer systems

What is a computer?

computer	computer/desktop
supercomputer	tower case
mainframe	laptop
minicomputer	notebook
workstation	subnotebook
PC (personal computer)	handheld computer/
microcomputer	palmtop/personal
Mac/Apple Macintosh	digital assistant/
Mac user/PC user	pocket computer
desktop	portable

A **computer** can be described as an electronic machine which can be used to store, process and display data. There are many different types of computer:

○ A **supercomputer** is extremely powerful. It can be used for very complex tasks, such as computer modelling of weather systems. These computers are extremely expensive, and are generally used by educational or scientific institutions, rather than individual users.

○ A **mainframe** is a powerful computer which is capable of processing large amounts of data, often enabling many people to use it, and to carry out many tasks, at the same time. A network of smaller computers or terminals is used to access the files and programs on the mainframe. Mainframes are therefore described as multi-user, multi-tasking machines.

○ A **minicomputer** is a multi-processing computer which is less powerful than a mainframe. It can also be used at the centre of a network of smaller computers.

○ A smaller computer in a network connected to a mainframe, or other more powerful computer, is often called a **workstation**. A workstation may, however, also be a relatively powerful computer, usually with good graphics capabilities, that may be either attached to a network or used as a stand-alone machine. The word is also used to refer to the physical place where a user works with a computer, usually at a desk.

○ A small computer designed to be used by an individual, for example at home or in an office, is sometimes called a **PC**, or **personal computer**. This kind of machine used to be called a **microcomputer**.

PC, or **personal computer**, is often used to refer to a personal computer which is not an Apple Macintosh machine. Apple Macintosh machines are known as **Macs**. This can be confusing, as Macs are also personal computers. However the distinction is often made between **Mac users**, and **PC users**.

a desktop computer with a tower case   *tower case*

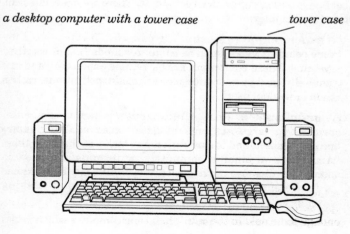

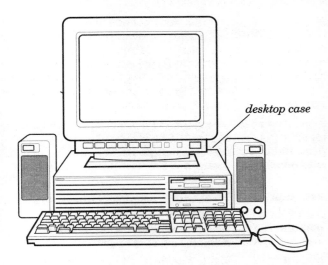

desktop case

○ Another type of personal computer is a **desktop** or **desktop computer**. This is a very common model, which as the name suggests, fits on a desk. Many users have desktop computers either at home, at work or in educational institutions. A desktop is not designed to be portable, which means it does not have an independent power supply, and is too big and heavy to be carried easily.

Some people use the term 'desktop' to refer to the case which sits under the computer screen on a desk, distinguishing it from a **tower case**, which stands vertically next to the screen or on the floor.

○ A **laptop** is smaller than a desktop. Laptops are portable and can use batteries. As the name suggests, a laptop is small and light enough to fit on the user's lap (the horizontal area that is formed by your thighs when you sit down). A **notebook** is like a laptop, but is smaller, and a **subnotebook** is even smaller.

○ A **handheld computer**, sometimes called a **palmtop**, a **PDA (personal digital assistant)**, or a **pocket computer**, is small enough to be held in the user's hand.

3

a laptop computer

Dialogue

customer: Excuse me, I wonder if you could give me some advice.

assistant: Yes of course. Are you looking for anything in particular?

customer: Well, I'm not sure. I'd like to buy a computer to use at home.

assistant: Right. What sort of things do you want to use it for?

customer: Well, I'd like to be able to use it for writing letters and doing the household accounts, and my children want to play games. I'd like to try the Internet, especially the Web, and e-mail, too.

assistant: OK. Do you need a machine that you can carry around with you?

customer: You mean a portable?

assistant: Yes, a laptop, for example.

customer: I'm not sure. Aren't they a bit expensive?

assistant: Well, yes, they are a bit more expensive than desktops with the same specifications, but they're much more affordable than they used to be.

customer: I see. Well, I still think I should look at your desktop computers first.

4

All these small light computers can be called **portables**, as they can be carried around and used when the mains power supply is not available.

What is a computer system?

computer system	reboot
hardware	user name
software	user ID
input	login name
output	password
platform	log in/on
boot up	

A computer is just a machine, but a **computer system** consists of two main elements: the machine and programs, or **hardware** and **software**. 'Hardware' refers to the physical components of the system. These components are mechanical and electronic. For more information about hardware, see chapter 2.

The central idea of a computing system is that **input** is processed into **output**. Input is the data which is entered into the computer, and output is the result of processing done by the computer, usually printed out or displayed on the screen.

Different computer systems can be called computer **platforms**. This refers to the combination of the machine and the operating system, for example a Pentium II running Windows 98. (This is explained in more detail in Chapter 8).

Software

software	applications software
program	freeware
systems software	shareware
operating system	courseware
utilities	

Software refers to the **programs** which are used on a computer system. A computer program is a set of commands which the computer understands and follows. These commands perform tasks which the user wants the computer to do.

Below are some words and phrases associated with starting up and connecting to a computer system:

boot up or **boot** to start a computer system (a system)

reboot (a system) to restart a computer system

user name
user ID the sequence of letters and/or
login name numbers which identifies you to a computer system

password a word or sequence of letters and/or numbers that you type in, in order to access programs or areas of a computer system

log in or **log on** to type in your user name, usually in combination with a password, in order to access a system as an authorized user

log off or **log out** to leave a computer system that you are currently logged on to.

-WARE

There are other terms related to computers which contain '-ware', in addition to **software** and **hardware**:

Freeware is software which is available free of charge. This can be found on the Internet, or perhaps in the form of a cover disk – a disk which comes free with a computing magazine. Sometimes people talk about 'free' software. In such cases, the word 'free' means that you may freely use it for your own purposes, such as in your own programs, if you are a software developer.

Shareware is software which is distributed free of charge, but is available to the user for only a limited time period, after which it must be paid for.

Courseware is software or data which is used as part of online learning, computer based training (CBT) or computer aided learning (CAL). See 'Educational' below.

Software is used for various functions. **Systems software** is used to run a computer system. It includes **operating systems** and **utilities** (see chapter 3).

○ An **operating system** is a piece of software which provides the user with a means of interacting with a computer, and co-ordinates the operations carried out by programs. An example of an operating system is Windows 98.

○ **Utilities** are programs which perform tasks that allow the system to operate smoothly, such as the organization of files.

○ The programs used for more complex tasks, such as word processing or e-mail are known as **applications software**.

The role of computers

The potential uses of computers are almost infinite, and this section mentions some of the most common current uses of computers in everyday life.

Personal

the Internet	CD-ROM
e-mail	PIM (personal information
computer games	manager)
multimedia	

Computers have many uses for individuals. People use the **Internet** (see chapter 9) to explore their personal hobbies and interests, and to find information on an enormous variety of topics. It is also becoming increasingly common to access goods and services via the Internet, using it to book a holiday, or to order CDs and books online, for example. Users also use the Internet to make contact, and keep in touch with people all over the world using **e-mail**.

In the world of leisure, **computer games** are popular, and **multi-media** (using more than one medium, such as text plus audio or video) **CD-ROMs** (see chapter 2) are used for both leisure and education. People using home computers also use **PIMs** (**personal information managers**) to organize personal information such as addresses, to write notes and to write lists of tasks to do.

Educational

word-processing program	virtual reality
databases	CAL (computer-assisted
distance learning	learning)
online learning	CBT (computer-based
virtual classroom	training)

In schools, colleges and universities, students use **word-processing programs** to write essays and projects, and use **databases** to find books and information. The Internet is also an important educational tool, and is used in **distance learning**. Other common uses of computers in education are e-mail, which enables the academic community to make and maintain contacts worldwide, and **online learning**, which uses the Internet as a medium for instruction

Dialogue

student:	Hello, could you help me please?
librarian:	Yes of course. What can I do for you?
student:	I need some information about the computing facilities here.
librarian:	OK. Well, you can use the PCs on the second floor, and there's also a Mac lab on the third floor. There are word-processing and various other programs available on those machines, and you can print there too. You'll need to apply for a password first before you can log on.
student:	Great. And can I get access to the Internet and e-mail as well?
librarian:	Yes, your department will set up an e-mail account for you.
student:	OK, that's fine. Also, how can I search for books using the computers?
librarian:	You can do that using the online catalogue, which is a database of all the books and articles in the library. You can also use it to search the catalogues of other libraries.
student:	OK, that's really helpful. Thanks very much.

and educational development. The **virtual classroom** is a concept used in online learning. It refers to a classroom which exists in the virtual space of the Internet.

CD-ROMs may be used in **computer-based training** (**CBT**). **Computer-assisted learning** (**CAL**) is an increasingly common way for people to approach education.

The term **virtual reality** refers to a type of reality which is conceptual and non-physical. The word **virtual** is used to describe contexts which exist in a non-physical computing dimension. For example:

virtual classroom   a computer-based learning environment in which students and tutors can interact

virtual bookshop   a website where users can order books

Commercial

e-commerce   graphics program
spreadsheet program   database

E-commerce (business conducted on the Internet) is becoming more widespread. Through its website (see chapter 9), a company can offer computer users the opportunity to order and pay for goods and services using their credit cards on the Internet.

Many companies use **spreadsheet programs** to do their accounts, and word processing has replaced the use of traditional typewriters in many offices. Computers and **graphics programs** are extremely important in professions such as publishing and advertising. Companies can also use computers to compile **databases** of clients, for example. PIMs (personal information managers) are also commonly used in business, enabling users to make notes, arrange appointments, and index names and other details of business contacts. Different types of program are covered in Chapters 5 and 6.

Computers have allowed companies to reduce the amount of paper they use, to deal with information more efficiently, and to exchange

Dialogue

Two managers are discussing how the installation of a new computer system has changed the way one of their companies is run.

manager 1: So tell me about your new computer system. Has it made a difference to your company?

manager 2: It's actually made a huge difference.

manager 1: In what way?

manager 2: Well, we're able to publicize and sell our products on our website, which has been quite successful. We're using e-mail a lot to communicate with our overseas clients as well, which is a lot quicker than normal mail.

manager 1: Great. What else have you changed?

manager 2: We're using a database program to store information about clients. That's really useful, as we can search it quickly for the information that we need.

manager 1: Maybe I should come and have a look.

manager 2: No problem!

and publish data more easily. Theoretically, computers reduce the amount of paper used in an office, although many people argue that printing is now so easy that more paper is used in the office than ever before.

2

Hardware

Hardware refers to the mechanical and electronic aspects of a computer system – the parts you can touch. This chapter looks at the **basic components** involved, along with **expansion boards** – the extra elements which can be added to a computer to expand its capabilities – and **peripherals**, which are separate elements attached to the computer.

Basic components

> chip
> integrated circuit
> CPU (central processing unit)
> printed circuit board
> motherboard
> clock speed
> megahertz (MHz)
>
> memory
> ROM (read only memory)
> RAM (random access memory)
> main memory
> volatile/non-volatile
> megabyte (Mb)
> CD-ROM

Chips

The most essential part of a computer is a **chip**, which is a very small piece of silicon, or other semi-conducting material, that contains a complex electrical circuit called an **integrated circuit**. The most important chip in a computer is called the **CPU**, or **central processing unit** or a **microprocessor**. This chip is seen as the 'brain' of the computer, as it does most of the computer's processing, although many other chips are essential. The CPU is found on a **printed circuit board**, which is a flat plastic sheet, holding the electronic components. The board which holds the CPU is called the **motherboard**. The speed at which a computer operates is highly dependent on the power of the CPU. This speed is called the **clock speed** and is measured in **megahertz (MHz)** – millions of operations per second.

Memory

Memory is the part of the computer which stores data and commands. This is a very complex area of computing, and there are many different types of memory, but two useful terms for the general user are **ROM** (**read only memory**) and **RAM** (**random access memory**). RAM refers to the memory held in chips, and is also known as the **main memory**. This memory is part of the system resources of the computer, and the amount of this memory influences the speed and capacity of the machine. RAM is described as **volatile**, as data can be lost from it if the power is switched off. It is measured in **megabytes** (**Mbs**), sometimes informally called 'megs'.

ROM is a permanent part of the computer's memory which cannot be changed. ROM is described as **non-volatile**, as the information is not lost if the power is switched off.

Storage devices

storage devices	**optical drive/disk**
hard drive/disk	**CD-R**
floppy drive/disk	**CD-RW**
zip drive/disk	**DVD**
back up	**backup tape**
create backups	

There are various **storage devices** which can be used to hold data.

○ A magnetic disk inside the computer, called the **hard disk**, may be used.

○ Data can also be stored in a portable format using a **floppy disk** (or **floppy**), which is a small disk contained in a plastic case. A single floppy disk holds much less data than the hard disk of a computer, but can be removed and used in any computer with a **floppy drive**.

○ A **zip disk** is another storage device which, like a floppy disk, allows the user to store data in a portable form. However, zip disks are different from floppy disks as they hold a much larger quantity of data. A **zip drive** can be either an internal, permanent part of a computer, or external and portable. A portable zip drive can be connected to any computer. Users very often use floppies or zip disks to **back up** (make a copy of) data they have stored on the hard disk of a computer.

○ An even larger quantity of data can be held on an optical disk, such as a CD-ROM (a disk which you buy with data already recorded on it), a CD-R (a disk on which you can record data), a CD-RW (a rewritable disk), or a DVD (digital versatile disk or digital video disk).

○ Finally, **backup tapes** are commonly used for saving network data and making archives. Backup tapes use electromagnetism to record data, and can hold huge amounts of information. They are however, much slower than optical disks.

Creating backups is an important security measure, since there is always the possibility that data may be lost from one storage device.

Dialogue

student:	Oh no! I don't believe it.
teacher:	What's the matter?
student:	I think I've just accidentally deleted a file.
teacher:	Really? Have you got a backup?
student:	No. That's the problem. I forgot to back it up onto a floppy. I just saved it onto the hard disk.
teacher:	That's a pity! You should back up all your files every week onto a zip disk.
student:	Ah well, you live and learn...

Expansion boards

card	graphics/video card
expansion board	network card
adapter	modem
expansion slot	install
add on	put in
sound card	fit

The capabilities of a computer can be expanded by adding further boards which enable the computer to perform specialized functions. These less essential boards are often called **cards**, or **adapters**, and can be put into **expansion slots** (sockets that expansion boards fit into). They are also called **add-ons**, as they are elements which can be added on to a computer system.

○ A **sound card** can be installed, which enables the user to hear sound through speakers or headphones, and to record sound using a microphone.

○ A **graphics card**, or **video card** can enable the computer to display graphics or video on the screen.

○ A **network card** is an add-on which allows the user to connect the computer to a local network of computers.

○ A **modem** is another piece of hardware which is used to connect

Dialogue

Mel is telling Liz about her plans to upgrade her computer.

Mel: I'm upgrading my machine next week.

Liz: Are you? What are you going to do?

Mel: Well, I've got three spare expansion slots, so I'm going to put in another 32 megabytes of RAM.

Liz: 32 megs? That should make your machine a lot faster. What else are you planning?

Mel: I'm going to install a sound card so that I can download music from the Web.

Liz: That sounds good.

Mel: And I'm thinking about putting in a new graphics card too, so that I can play some new games.

an individual computer to the Internet via a telephone line
(discussed in more detail in chapter 9).

Various verbs are used to talk about adding new hardware
elements to a computer system. The most common are
install, **put in** and **fit**.

Examples:

*I bought a new computer, and the shop **installed** the modem
for me.*

*This machine is so much faster now I've **put in** extra memory.*

*I'd like to **fit** a new sound card.*

Note: More details on adding software are given in chapter 6.

Peripherals

This word is potentially confusing as it is sometimes used to refer
to *non-essential* elements of a computer system. However, it is also
sometimes used to talk about elements of a system which are *physically separate* from the main unit. According to the first meaning,
the keyboard, for example, would not be seen as a peripheral,
whereas according to the second meaning it would. This section
uses the second meaning, and so refers to elements which are
external to the main unit, but are connected to it. These can be
classified into two groups – **input devices** and **output devices**.

Input devices

peripheral	mouse mat
input device	pointer
to input	I-beam pointer
output device	selection pointer
keyboard	touchpad
scanner	graphics
scan in	tablet/digitizing
microphone	tablet
pointing device	light pen
mouse	joystick
pointing stick	tracker ball
mouse pad	

input devices

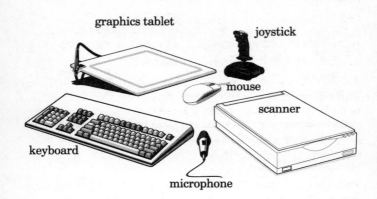

graphics tablet

joystick

mouse

scanner

keyboard

microphone

output devices

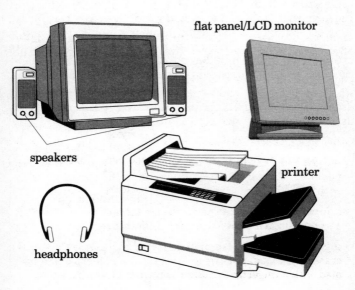

flat panel/LCD monitor

speakers

printer

headphones

Input devices, as the name suggests, are used to put in, or enter, data.

One of the most important input devices is the **keyboard**. Users can type in text using the keyboard, which looks very similar to the keys of a traditional typewriter, or can enter keyboard commands (which are covered in chapter 4).

Another device which can be used to **input** data is a **scanner**. This electronic device is used to transfer an image such as text, or pictures, into the computer. It is possible to **scan in** any image, store it and view it on the screen. Another way to input data is to use a **microphone** (in the case of audio data, such as speech or music), or when using voice recognition software to, for example, dictate to a word-processing program.

Pointing devices allow the user to point to elements on the screen. The most useful pointing device is a **mouse** – a small electronic device that is normally attached to the computer by means of a thin cable. It is operated using the hand on a small mat called a **mouse mat** or **mouse pad**. The mouse gets its name from the fact that it looks like a mouse with a tail. This is used to control the position of the **pointer** on the screen, which generally appears as either a small vertical line (known as an **I-beam pointer**) or an arrow (known as a **selection pointer**). Laptop computers often have a **touchpad** on the keyboard which the user can use to direct the pointer on the screen by moving a finger across the pad. A **graphics tablet** (or **digital tablet** or **tablet**) is a device which functions like an electronic pen and paper. The user can draw on its flat surface with a special 'pen' or 'stylus', and the drawings are transferred onto the screen.

Other input devices include:

○ **a light pen**: acts like a mouse, but allows the user to move the pointer and to select objects on the screen by pointing at them with the light pen, which uses a light-sensitive detector

○ **a joystick**: similar to the device a pilot holds when flying an aeroplane, often used for playing computer games

○ **a pointing stick**: a miniature joystick the size of a pencil's eraser tip, situated between the keys of a notebook, and operated with a fingertip to move the pointer on the screen

○ **a tracker ball**: a ball moved by the user's palm or fingers to move the pointer on the screen

Output devices

monitor	resolution
screen	dumb terminal
VDU (visual display unit)	printer
	hard copy
CRT (cathode ray tube)	speakers
flat panel/LCD monitor	headphones

Several devices are used to display the output from a computer.

A **monitor** is an item of equipment with a **screen**. A monitor is sometimes called a **VDU**, or **visual display unit**. There are two main types of **display screen**. The first, the **CRT** (**cathode ray tube**), is most commonly used on desks in offices. It is quite large, and rather like a conventional TV. The second, the **flat panel** (or **LCD monitor**) is slim, takes up little space, and uses the same technology as that used for screens on laptop computers or notebooks. The quality of images on a screen is measured in terms of **resolution**, with high resolution monitors generally being capable of displaying text and images with greater clarity.

A **dumb terminal** is a combination of VDU and keyboard without any processing power. Instead, it is connected to a central computer on which all programs are run.

Another important output device is the **printer**, which allows the user to produce paper copies of data held in the computer, known as **hard copy**.

Speakers and **headphones** allow the listener to hear audio data, such as speech or music, through the computer

Abbreviations:

CPU is pronounced as individual letters /si: pi: ˈ juː/

VDU is pronounced /vi: di: ˈ juː/

CRT is pronounced /si: ɑ: ˈti: /

RAM and **ROM** are pronounced as words, not individual letters.

pointer and cursor

The terms **pointer** and **cursor** are often used interchangeably, though sometimes a distinction is made between them. An arrow that moves on the screen when you move the mouse (or other pointing device) is called a **pointer**, **mouse pointer** or **selection pointer** (or **arrow**), and the solid rectangle or blinking underline character that indicates where the next character you type will appear on the screen is called the **cursor**. Sometimes, text processors use a special pointer (or cursor) called an **I-beam pointer**, that appears as a vertical line like a capital 'I', between characters. This identifies the point at which text may be inserted.

3

Systems software

This chapter looks at software which runs computer systems.

User interfaces and operating systems

command line user interface	Linux
graphical user interface	Mac OS
(GUI)	Microsoft Windows
point-and-click interface	OS/2
MS-DOS	multi-user system
Unix	multi-tasking system

In order to use a computer, a user needs to be able to communicate with it, and give it instructions. The are two main ways in which users communicate with computers. One is via a **command line user interface**, and the other is through a **graphical user interface**, also known as a **point-and-click interface**.

Command line interfaces

A **command line interface** requires the user to instruct the computer by typing in commands. The following operating systems (or 'OSs', pronounced /oʊˈɛsɪz/) have a command line interface.

o **MS-DOS** (**Microsoft disk operating system**): an operating system used for IBM or IBM-compatible computers; pronounced /ɛmɛsˈdɒs/. Under Windows 95 and 98, you can move to the 'DOS prompt', which uses the same command line interface, and accepts the same commands as the DOS operating system. Windows 95 and 98 are actually operating systems in their own right, and the DOS prompt is really a simulation of DOS as an operating system.

o **Unix**: a very powerful and reliable operating system which is often used in commercial and academic networks.

○ **Linux**: an 'Open Source' operating system (meaning it may be freely used, copied and developed), which has the characteristics of Unix; it can be used on a personal computer.

'DOS' can, strictly, refer to any operating system, but is often used to refer to MS-DOS.

Example from a command line user interface (MS-DOS), showing the result of entering the command 'dir', meaning 'list directory'.

```
① C:\WINDOWS>dir /p          ④        ⑦        ⑧
② SYMFOR   GRP          816   23/04/99   17:49
   INSTALL  LOG        3,574   22/07/97   16:19
   MICROSOF GRP ③      6,941   23/04/99   17:49
   CCARD200 EXE      127,424   02/03/94    0:00
   POWERPNT INI        1,967   04/07/98    9:10
   GRAPH5   INI          126   28/01/98   12:25
   ARTGALRY INI          218   28/01/98   12:25
   PLANET   BMP       46,478   23/06/98    0:02
   PLANET~1 BMP      274,556   26/03/98    4:36
   MSFFILE  INI          165   08/02/99   23:37
          425 file(s)    11,167,122 bytes ⑤
                          3,067,904 bytes free ⑥
⑨ C:\WINDOWS>
```

1 *command line*, 2 *file name*, 3 *file extension*, 4 *size of file*, 5 *total size of files in directory*, 6 *total space free on drive*, 7 *date on which file was last saved*, 8 *time at which files was last saved*, 9 *prompt showing the user where to enter commands*

Graphical user interfaces

A **graphical user interface** (or **GUI**, pronounced /ˈguːiː/) is different from a command line interface as it uses windows, icons, menus and pointers. The user can click on objects with the mouse, instead of typing in commands or using arrow keys. (See Chapter 4 for more details). This kind of interface is also known as a **'point-and-click' interface**.

There are various operating systems which can function in a graphical user interface. The most common are set out below:

○ **Mac OS**: the operating system used with Apple Macintosh machines.

○ **Microsoft Windows**: probably the most well-known and widely-used operating system; used with PCs. Examples of the various versions available are Windows 95, Windows 98 and Windows NT.

○ **OS/2**: IBM's own Windows-based operating system for use on PCs; it is compatible with both Windows and DOS.

Operating systems which allow a number of users using individual terminals to access a single machine at the same time are called **multi-user systems**. Similarly, systems which can run more than one program at the same time are known as **multi-tasking systems**.

An example of a graphical user interface (Microsoft Windows)

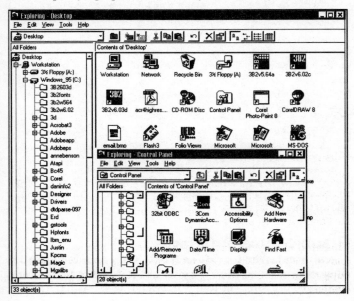

Utilities and basic procedures

---

utilities/utility programs	virus checker
	create
file management	save
disk maintenance	rename
compression	delete
directory/folder	copy
subdirectory/subfolder	move

Utilities or **utility programs** are programs which are used to organize and maintain a computer system. Many of them run 'in the background' without the user noticing them. Some utilities, however, respond to instructions from the user. The following section concentrates mainly on this category. Utilities are used to perform a variety of functions, for example:

○ file management

○ disk maintenance

○ creation of backups

○ file compression

○ virus checking

○ automation of tasks

File management

Files can be organized into **folders** and **sub-folders** or and **sub-directories** using programs like Windows Explorer. This software allows the user to create categories for files which can be organized and accessed easily.

This kind of program can be used to **create** and **save** files and folders. It is also possible to **rename** files and folders, **delete** them, **copy** them or **move** them from one area to another (see example overleaf).

Windows Explorer

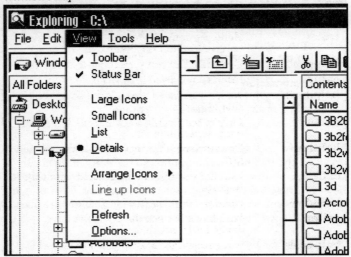

Verbs commonly used before 'a file':

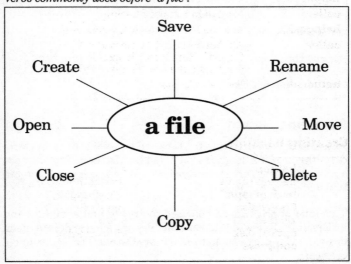

Dialogue

caller:	Hello. I wonder if you can help me. I seem to have lost an important file.
helpdesk:	Certainly. Did you remember to save it?
caller:	I think so. I saved it in Word.
helpdesk:	Well, if you saved it as a Word document it should be there.
caller:	I know, but I can't see it. I think the file name was 'Report 2'.
helpdesk:	Do you remember which folder you put it in?
caller:	I think I put it in a folder called 'Monthly Reports'.
helpdesk:	Have you tried looking in Explorer?
caller:	Yes I have. It's not there. I must have deleted it by accident.
helpdesk:	Not necessarily. Maybe you just moved it into a different folder.
caller:	I'm sure I saved it in 'Monthly Reports'.
helpdesk:	Did you copy it onto a floppy?
caller:	No. I didn't make a backup.
helpdesk:	Are you sure you didn't rename it?
caller:	Ah! You're right! I renamed it 'New Report'. Here it is. I'll open it and check ... yes, that's the file. Thanks very much.
helpdesk:	You're welcome.

Creating backups

backup	zip
backup media	defragmentation ('defragging')
backup tape	swap file
floppy disk	virus
zip disk	virus checker
optical disk	
compress	

25

Utilities are also used to create **backups**, which are extra copies of files. Users create backups just in case original files are lost, as a result of human error or system failure. Backups can be created in various ways. **Backup media** include:

o **backup tapes**

o **floppy disks**

o **zip disks**

o **optical disks** (eg. CD-ROMs)

Files saved by users on a network drive (ie. on a server) are usually backed up automatically. All the above are described in Chapter 2.

File compression

It is possible to **compress** or **zip** files, so that they use less space. This can be useful, for example when sending files via e-mail. File compression programs such as WinZip can be used to do this.

Disk maintenance

Utilities can be used to help the hard disk function efficiently.

One process which is performed by utility programs is **defragmentation**, or '**defragging**'. This refers to the reorganization of data on a disk, so that files are stored as continuous units, enabling them to be read by the computer more easily.

Computers can work more quickly when they have more memory available. When a computer is processing data, it uses a utility called a **swap file**. This is a file which the computer uses to store information which it does not need for its immediate task. By storing information in this separate file, more memory is freed for the processing task it is working on. It is called a 'swap' file, as the contents of this file are constantly swapped, or exchanged, depending on whether they are needed by the computer at that moment or not.

Virus checking

Viruses are coded instructions which are designed deliberately to cause problems in a computer system. They are sometimes hidden in programs, or in innocent-looking files, and are not obvious to users. They can enter a computer system via an e-mail attachment, or on a floppy disk that has been used in an infected machine, for example. Virus checkers are an important type of utility program which search for viruses on the computer, and can destroy them. An example of a virus checker is Doctor Solomon's Anti Virus Toolkit.

Automating tasks

batch file	**optimizer**
cron job	**encryption tools**
macro	**screensaver**
diagnostic tools	**uninstaller**

Many of the tasks performed by utility programs can be automated to make them faster and easier for the user. It is also possible for users to set up automated routines by using:

○ **batch files**

If a user is working within a command line interface, it is possible to enter a sequence of commands and save them as a **batch file**, with the file extension '.bat'. The word 'batch' means 'a group', and refers to the group of commands typed in by the user. When the user activates this file, the computer will obey the sequence of commands. This is used for common sequences of commands, and is a useful way of saving time.

○ **cron jobs** (Unix/Linux)

If the user is working with a Unix or Linux operating system, it is possible to set up a **cron job**. This is a processing job which can be set up to begin while the user is not present, for example in the middle of the night. Examples of tasks which might be performed using a cron job might be defragging the hard disk, or backing up certain sets of files.

○ **macros**

To automate a series of tasks within an application, users can create a macro. A macro is a recording of a series of operations. It can be activated and will perform this series of operations as a single unit. This allows the user to do the job more quickly and easily, by activating the macro instead of performing all the operations separately. Macros can be activated using a short-cut key or combination of keys on the keyboard, by clicking on a button on a toolbar, or by selecting a command in a drop-down menu. They are particularly useful for common tasks which require a long and complicated sequence of keystrokes and/or menu options.

---

create a batch file

set up a batch file

I'm going to set up a batch file to automate all these minor operations.

create a cron job

set up a cron job

I've created a cron job to process the data overnight.

create a macro

set up a macro

record a macro

Why don't you record a macro instead of entering all those commands over and over again?

run a batch file

run a cron job

run a macro

We can save time by running a batch file.

The following are also sometimes regarded as utilities:

○ **diagnostic tools and optimizers**: programs which identify problems on a system, and suggest ways of making the best use of resources.

○ **security and encryption tools**: for example, programs which translate e-mail messages into a special form, making them readable only to those who possess a special 'key'.

○ **screensavers**: programs that cause activity on the screen when the user has not been working on the computer for some time; this prevents damage to the screen.

○ **uninstallers**: programs that safely uninstall (remove) other programs, making sure that elements used by existing programs are not deleted.

4

Introduction to applications software

applications software	program
software package	suite
application	

In order to use computers to perform such tasks as writing letters or creating reports, users need **applications software** or **software packages** – programs or groups of programs which have been designed for particular types of task, such as word processing. These programs are called **applications**, as they are examples of computing technology applied to specific tasks. In everyday language, people often refer to applications or packages as **programs**. A **suite** is a group of applications which are designed to work well with each other, and are often sold together, such as Microsoft Office, or Lotus SmartSuite.

For more details on buying and installing software, see chapter 6.

Dialogue

customer:	I'm planning to buy a new computer, and I want to update my word-processing program.
shop assistant:	Well, we sell that one as part of a whole suite of applications that comes with the new computer.
customer:	What other programs does it include?
shop assistant:	There's an e-mail package, a spreadsheet program, a presentations package and a database application.

Common features of applications

Although applications may be designed for different purposes, they are becoming increasingly similar in appearance, and in the way in which they are used. This enables users to learn how to work with different programs easily. Most applications allow the user to select commands by clicking on icons and menus, instead of entering commands using the keyboard only. Such applications have many features in common.

Appearance of data on screen

Many applications that run in a graphical user interface environment (see chapter 3) are said to be 'WYSIWYG' applications. This means that they display files on the screen in the same way as they will print on paper. WYSIWYG stands for 'what you see is what you get', and is pronounced 'wizzy-wig'.

Menu

(drop-down) menu	**radio button**
click	**alert box**
drop-down list	**double-click**
select (1)	**right-click**
dialogue box	**click and drag**
text box	**shift click**

On the screen, there is very often a list of **menus** listed horizontally near the top. A menu is like a menu in a restaurant; it offers a list of choices. The menus have titles indicating their general function. A possible list of menus is:

File Edit View Insert Format Tools Table Window Help

Each of these menus offers a list of options. In order to open a menu, the user **clicks** on the word, by placing the mouse pointer over it and pressing the left-hand button. This causes the list of choices to 'drop down' from the word. For this reason they are sometimes called **drop-down menus**. Here is an example from a popular word-processing program.

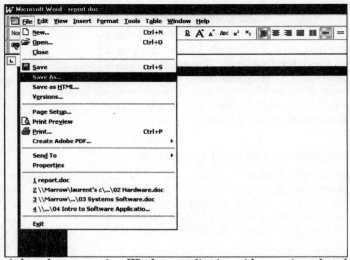

A drop-down menu in a Windows application with an option selected

Another type of menu is the **drop-down list**, which appears when the user clicks on a downward-pointing arrow on a toolbar, for example the list showing font sizes.

To choose options from menus and lists, you have to **click** on (or **select**) the option that you want. For example, in order to open a file in a word-processing package, you click on the 'File' menu, and then click on 'Open'. A **dialogue box** then appears on your screen, which allows you to choose which file you want to open. It is called a 'dialogue' box because it allows you to have a dialogue, or to communicate, with the computer.

It is common for **dialogue box** to be written as **dialog box**, because many software companies use American English.

Dialogue boxes contain **text boxes** for the user to type in, and **radio buttons**, which are small circular areas that can be clicked on.

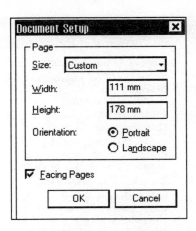

dialogue box with text boxes and radio buttons

An **alert box** is another type of message, used to warn the user about a potential problem.

---

expressions with *click*

click	You **click** on an element of the screen when you move your mouse pointer over it, and press the mouse button, usually the left one.
double-click	You **double-click** when you click twice quickly.
right-click	If you have two buttons on your mouse, you can **right-click**, using the right-hand button. Right-clicking produces a menu of choices.
click and drag	You **click and drag** with the mouse when you select an element of the file by clicking and moving the mouse pointer across it, holding your finger down on the button.
shift-click	You **shift-click** when you hold down the shift key and click. You can select everything in the file between the cursor and the mouse pointer.

Dialogue

user:	How do I open a document in Word?
helpdesk:	Go to the 'File' menu and click on 'Open'. A dialogue box will appear. Click on the name of the file you want.
user:	I want to delete a complete paragraph in this document. How can I do it quickly?
helpdesk:	Select the paragraph by clicking and dragging the mouse over it. Then press the 'delete' key on your keyboard.
user:	Thanks. And how do I move the paragraph?
helpdesk:	Select the paragraph. Then click on the 'Cut' button. Next, paste it in by clicking on the point where you want to insert it, then clicking on the 'Paste' button.

Dialogue

user:	Could you tell me how to insert a table into a Word document?
helpdesk:	Yes. Open up the 'Table' menu, and click on 'Insert Table'.
user:	OK.
helpdesk:	Can you see the dialogue box headed 'Insert Table'?
user:	Yes.
helpdesk:	Right, how many columns and rows do you want in your table?
user:	Four columns and four rows.
helpdesk:	OK. Click on the little arrow pointing up, in the box indicating 'number of columns'. Choose 'four'. Do the same in the box indicating 'Number of rows'. Then click on 'OK'. That's it.
user:	Thanks very much.

Toolbars

toolbar	**Control key**
button	**Alt key**
icon	**keystroke**
floating toolbar	**hot-key combination**
hot key	

In addition to the menus, many applications have one or more **toolbars** near the top of the application window.

A toolbar is usually a horizontal strip showing small squares, called **buttons**. Each button has a small picture, or **icon**, on it which represents the function of the button. For example, the 'Cut' button shows a pair of scissors. Toolbar buttons cover various functions: for example, you can save a document by clicking on the 'Save' button, which has an icon of a floppy disk on it. The function of each button can often be seen in written form by placing the mouse pointer over the button without clicking on it. A small caption will appear describing its function, for example 'Save'.

Some toolbars are vertical, and are situated at the side of an application window. Others may be situated anywhere the user places them on the screen. This kind of toolbar is called a **floating toolbar**.

Most functions performed by toolbars can also be performed using drop-down menus. The advantage of the toolbar is that it is quicker and easier to use. For this reason the toolbar contains the most commonly used commands.

Keyboard commands (hot keys)

In addition to using the mouse to perform operations within an application, it is also possible to use the keyboard to give the computer commands. This is usually done in a Windows environment by pressing the **Control key**, which is marked 'Ctrl', and sometimes the '**Alt**' (pronounced /alt/ or /ɔːlt/) **key**, together with another key or keys. The keys which can be used in this way are sometimes called **hot keys**, and the sequence of **keystrokes** resulting is called a **hot-key combination**. Here are some of the most commonly used keyboard commands:

These hot keys are used when an element of the file, such as text, a row, a table or a graphic has been 'selected', (see 'Editing Files', chapter 5):

Ctrl+C = Copy   (copies the text selected)

Ctrl+X = Cut   (cuts out the text selected)

Ctrl+V = Paste   (inserts the selection, which has been copied or cut from another location)

Ctrl+B   (makes selected text bold)

Ctrl+I   (makes selected text italic)

Ctrl+U   (underlines selected text)

The following commands do not require an element to be selected:

Ctrl+S = Save   (saves the file)

Ctrl+O = Open   (opens the file)

Ctrl+Alt+Delete   (closes down a running application and gives the user the option to restart the computer)

The scrollbar

scrollbar	**scroll through**
scroll up	**scroll left**
scroll down	**scroll right**

Another feature which is common to many applications is the **scrollbar**, which can be found on the right vertical edge of the application window. By clicking on the 'up' and 'down' arrows, or by using the mouse to drag the slider up or down, the user can **scroll up** or **scroll down** to view different parts of a file. You **scroll through** a document when you move through it, usually from beginning to end, using the scrollbar (or using the arrow keys, or the Page Up/Page Down keys).

Some applications also have a horizontal scrollbar along the bottom of the window, allowing the user to **scroll left** or **scroll right**.

Dialogue

student: I've typed in the text, but it keeps disappearing off to the right of the screen.

teacher: Well, you can either use the scrollbar at the bottom to scroll across to the right and see what you've written ...

student: Oh yes, I see.

teacher: ... or you can use the zoom control to view more of the document in the window.

student: How do I do that?

teacher: Click on the little arrow next to the box in the toolbar that says '100%' at the moment, and choose another value. Try 75%.

student: Oh, right. That's perfect.

5

Applications software: text and image processing

This chapter looks at several types of software which are primarily concerned with processing text and images (although they include other functions).

Text editors, HTML editors and word-processing packages

DTP (desktop publishing)	**delete**
edit	**click**
format (verb)	**double-click**
format (noun)	**click and drag**
formatting	**bold**
select (2)	**italic**
mark (up)	**underline**
highlight	**bullet**
copy	**font**
cut	**point size**
clipboard	**heading**
paste	**style**
drag and drop	

These types of application are similar in that they allow the user to enter and save text. Text editors are the most basic, as they only allow plain text to be entered and displayed. HTML editors and word-processing software allow the user to change the appearance of the text, and they can work with tables, charts, and graphics (pictures). In addition, HTML editors let the user include sound and video files. For more information on HTML, see chapter 7 (pages 60 and 61). **DTP** or **desktop publishing** packages give yet more control over formatting and page layout, allowing users to produce higher-quality and more sophisticated documents than they can with an ordinary word-processing package.

The next section looks at some of the language associated with editing – changing or modifying text or data in files – using these types of application.

Editing files

The appearance of the contents of files can be altered in a variety of ways using **editing** techniques. This process of changing the appearance of a document displayed in an application window is often called **formatting**.

---

expressions with *format*:

format (*verb*)

1 You **format** the contents of a file when you make adjustments which change its appearance, for example changing the font, adding tables, using numbers or bullets.

2 You can also **format** a disk. This means that you prepare it for reading and writing data. When you buy a computer, the hard disk is nearly always formatted and ready for use. Many floppies are also pre-formatted for use on, for example a PC or a Mac.

format (*noun*)

1 The **format** of a word-processed document is its layout or appearance.

2 From a more technical point of view, the **format** of a file is the file type: it may be a text file or a Word document, or a particular type of graphics file. **Native** file formats are those that are associated with a particular application. Doc files, for example, are native to Word.

formatting (*noun*) A file that contains a lot of **formatting** contains a lot of features, such as tables, numbers, bullets, bold, italic, underlining, etc.

In a word-processing program, you can choose which parts of the text you want to edit by **selecting**, **marking**, **marking up**, or **highlighting** (see screenshot on page 41). All these terms have the same meaning in this context. Once you have selected a section,

Dialogue

user: I've finished the report you asked us to type.

trainer: Right. Now you need to format it, so that the lists are numbered and the headings are in bold.

Dialogue

user: Shall I save this article now?.

trainer: Yes. But it contains a lot of formatting, so make sure you've got enough space on your disk.

Dialogue

user: What do you think of the letter I typed?

trainer: Well, I like the format, but there are a few grammatical mistakes that you'll need to correct.

you can **copy** it or **cut** it. These operations put it on the **clipboard**, an area where files or sections of files can be temporarily stored until they are pasted into another file, or a different part of the same file. Elements are moved around a document by **cutting and pasting** (see chapter 4), or **dragging and dropping** (selecting an area of text, moving it with the mouse, and then releasing it). Alternatively, the selected part can be **deleted**. This means that it is taken out permanently.

If you **click** three times quickly on the left of the screen in Word, you select the whole file. A single paragraph can be highlighted by **double-clicking** to the left of it. A single click on the left of the screen selects a line, and a single word can be marked by double clicking on it. Alternatively, a section of text can be selected by **clicking and dragging** the mouse pointer across it. When an element of a file has been selected, a black background appears behind it and the text becomes white, as can be seen in this example.

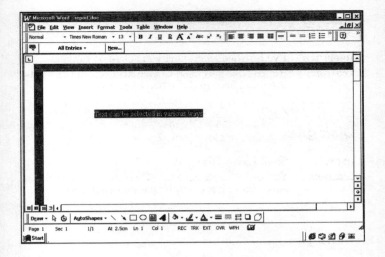

After selecting text, it is possible to change its appearance. This can be done using the **formatting toolbar**, which contains buttons and drop-down menus for performing the common formatting tasks. For example, it can be used to make text **bold**, *italic* or <u>underlined</u>. You can also use it to create a numbered list or a list marked with **bullets**:

○ This is an example of a bullet.

The size and style of text in a file is dictated by the **font**, which can be made smaller or larger using the 'Font Size' list on the toolbar. The size of text is often expressed as a number, called its **point size**.

It is also possible to choose between a large number of fonts, in different styles. Times New Roman and Arial are probably the most popular, but there are many more, for example:

Helvetica, Courier, *Script*, Book Antiqua,
Modern, Roman, Terminal

As well as allowing you to change the font, word-processing programs allow you to use automatic **headings**, like these:

Heading 1

Heading 2

Heading 3

Headings are examples of **styles**. These are special ways of formatting text, which the user can set up in advance to give the different elements of a document a consistent appearance.

Other features of word-processing programs

align	**spellcheck(er)**
justify	**Page Setup**
table of contents	**margin**
index	**Print Preview**
word count	**macro**

It is possible to change the appearance of large blocks of text. They can be **aligned** to the left, the centre or the right, and can be **justified**, which means that the text is spaced out to fill the line.

○ An automatic **table of contents** can be produced in a word-processing program, by using the 'Insert' menu. It also allows you to compile **indexes**.

○ If you want to find out how many words you have written, you can **do a word count**, and you can also check for spelling mistakes by **running the spellchecker** (see Appendix B).

○ The **Page Setup** can be adjusted, altering the appearance of the page. For example the size of the **margins**, which are the spaces at the edges of the text, can be changed.

○ Before printing a file, it is possible to see what it will look like on the page using **Print Preview**.

○ If the user has a long series of commands which are used very often, it can be useful to record a **macro**. A macro is a sequence of commands stored as a unit. This sequence can be activated by calling up the macro. A macro can be made available on a toolbar, or may be accessed via a keyboard command. (See chapter 3 for more details about macros.)

File formats

There are various types of file, which are identified by their **file extensions**. These are the groups of letters preceded by a dot that follow a file name.

---

common file extensions and their meanings:

.txt   a text file, composed of plain, ordinary text without-formatting.

.doc   Microsoft Word's 'native' format (See section 'expressions with *format*', this chapter).

.rtf   rich text format; a 'rich text' file which can contain basic formatting.

.pdf   portable document format; a file most commonly found on the Web. The format was produced by a company called Adobe, and can only be read in a program called Acrobat Reader.

.ps   PostScript Format; a type of file which can be used by a number of different applications on different platforms, especially to print documents with formatted text and graphics.

Graphics

---

graphics	**chart**
graphics package	**bar chart**
presentation package	**pie chart**

There are many applications which include a **graphics** component. Some word-processing programs, for example, support graphics, allowing the user to draw pictures, or import them (copy them across) from another application. **Graphics packages** and **presentation packages** are applications which are designed to create, display and edit pictures.

Graphics features

This section looks at graphics features which are included in text-editing and other programs.

Charts

One common use of presentation graphics applications is to create **charts** to display data or information in a pictorial form. This facility is often included in word-processing applications, and is also available in spreadsheet, accounts and statistics programs. There is a wide range of charts which can be produced. Some common examples are **bar charts** and **pie charts**. Here are two examples showing the same data, produced in Word:

bar chart

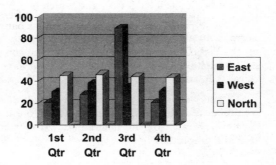

pie chart

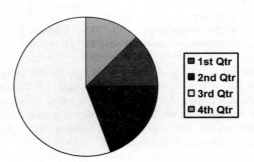

caller:	Hello. Could you tell me how to create a chart in Word?
helpdesk:	Of course. You click on the 'Insert Chart' button on the toolbar. It opens up a window that lets you to enter data into a spreadsheet and create charts from it. You can import the chart into your Word document.
caller:	That sounds quite simple. Does it only make bar charts?
helpdesk:	No. You can choose from a set of different types of chart, so you can create a bar chart, a pie chart, or whatever you want.
caller:	That's great. Thanks very much.
helpdesk:	You're welcome.

Drawings

Word-processing applications may include a drawing facility which allows the user to create and modify simple pictures. For example, it can create shapes:

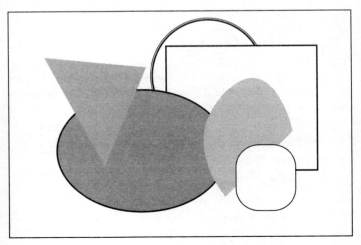

It can also be used to draw lines:

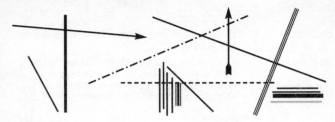

Graphics programs

paint program	customize
bit mapped graphics	scan in
vector graphics	CAD (computer-
draw program	assisted design)
palette	graphics tablet

This section looks at programs which are devoted only to graphics.

One type of graphics program is called a **paint program**. This is a program which allows the user to draw pictures and often edit images. All paint programs use **bitmapped graphics** (see 'file formats' below). Examples of such paint programs are Adobe Photoshop and PaintShop Pro. Programs which use **vector graphics** (see 'file formats' below) instead, for example CorelDraw, are often called **draw programs**.

The user can click on buttons in a toolbar to access more elements that give special effects, such as shadows around shapes. A **palette** of colours is provided, and the user may also be able to **customize** colours, in order to create different shades.

create a drawing

draw/paint a picture

make/create a chart

paste a chart into a file

import a picture/image into a file

an example from PaintShop Pro

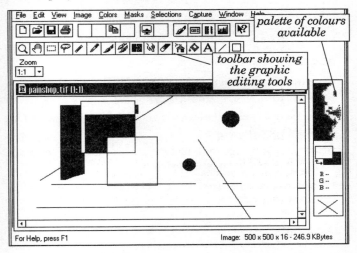

More advanced graphics programs, such as Adobe Photoshop allow the user to create more sophisticated images, potentially including the use of photographs. Photos can be **scanned in** (converted into a graphics file) and displayed on the screen. The user can also modify the appearance of photographs on the screen using this type of software.

A specialized type of software used by design professionals such as architects is **CAD** (**computer-assisted design**). A CAD system is a combination of hardware and software which is intended for use in design. A system like this includes specialist hardware, such as a **graphics tablet**, which is a device rather like an electronic pen and paper, used for drawing and for precision editing of images.

Tools

fill	**warp**
rubber stamp	**filter**
special effects	**transformation**

There is a wide variety of tools available on graphics programs.

47

Here are a few of the most common ones:

○ **fill**: a tool which allows the user to fill an area with a chosen colour.

○ **rubber stamp**: used to copy and repeat elements of an image in different areas of the screen.

○ **special effects**: used to create effects such as glows and reflections.

○ **warp**: used to change the shape of an image, for example making it appear curved.

○ **filter**: used to change the quality of the appearance of an image, for example making it appear sharper.

○ **transformations**: used to change images in various ways, for example changing the size of the picture, or rotating the picture.

File formats

BMP	PCX
JPEG	PNG
GIF	EPS
TIFF	PICT

There are many different file formats used in graphics programs. They can be split into two main groups: **bitmapped formats** and **vector formats**. The basic difference between the two is that bitmapped graphics (or 'raster graphics') become ragged when you reduce or increase them in size, whereas vector graphics (or 'object-oriented' graphics) increase or decrease in size smoothly:

bitmapped formats:

○ **Windows bitmap (.bmp)**: the standard bit mapped format used in Microsoft Windows.

○ **GIF (.gif**; usually pronounced /gɪf/): graphical interchange format; a compressed format used in web publishing.

○ **TIFF (.tif**; pronounced /tɪf/): tagged-image file format; a format for bitmapped images which can be used on PCs and Macs.

○ **PCX**: another widely-supported format for bitmapped images

○ **PNG** (**.png**; pronounced /pɪŋ/): portable network graphic; a versatile format used for web graphics.

vector formats:

○ **EPS**: uses a combination of PostScript command and either PICT or TIFF formats.

○ **PICT**: a standard graphics format on Macs.

Many files on the Web have a **.jpg** or **.jpeg** (pronounced /ˈdʒeɪpɛg/) extension. According to some, '**JPEG**' is not strictly a file format, but a compression technique. However, most people refer to it as a format.

Presentation packages

These applications are designed for people giving presentations. They allow the user to create 'slides' (images that can be projected) showing charts, diagrams, headings, text, bulleted lists, etc. These slides can be shown to an audience on a large screen, using a computer linked to a projector. In this sense they provide an electronic alternative to a traditional slide projector or overhead projector, although they are also commonly used to produce printed handouts or overhead transparencies to be used in presentations. An example of this type of program is PowerPoint.

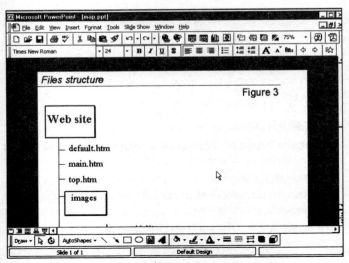

6

Applications software: data processing

This chapter looks at applications software which is used primarily for processing data. The main types of program covered are database programs and spreadsheet programs, in addition to a miscellaneous group of packages not already covered.

Database programs

database program	report
database management system	query (noun)
	query (verb)
field	sort
record	flatfile database
table	relational database
form	

A **database program**, or **database management system**, may be seen as an electronic filing system that is equivalent to a card index, but permits automated searches. It is an application which is used to store, maintain and access data. Database programs, such as Access, are very often used for large and complex data sets, such as a library catalogue, a store's inventory, or a company's customer records.

> The word **database** can be used to describe:
>
> ○ a large collection of data held on a computer (in one or many files)
>
> ○ a database program
>
> *We've set up a **database** of all the information we got from questionnaires we collected during the study.*
>
> *I know how to use a few computer programs – word processing, e-mail and **databases**.*

Databases use **fields** and **records** to organize data. A field is one category of information, and a record is a collection of fields. For example a record about a person may include fields such as name, date of birth, occupation, and address. Using the analogy of a card index, a record is equivalent to an individual card, a field is equivalent to a category of information that is common to all cards, and the database file is equivalent to the set of all cards. The data is displayed in the form of **tables**. A table may contain, for example, information about a selection of wines. The records would show the details about individual wines, usually shown horizontally in the table in rows. The fields would be information about the wine, such as its name, the vintage, the place of production, and so on. The field headings appear at the top of each column of the table.

WINE_ID	NAME	VINTAGE	CHATEAU
2	Valle di Vistalba Chardonnay	1996	Casa Nieto & Senetiner
3	Goyenechia Chardonnay	1997	Goyenechia
4	Navarro Correas Sauvignon Blanc	1995	Navarro Correas
5	Valle de Vistalba Malbec	1995	Casa Nieto & Senetiner
6	Goyenechia Cabernet Sauvignon	1996	Goyenechia
7	Nottage Hill Chardonnay	1996	Nottage Hill
8	Orlando RF Chardonnay	1996	Orlando RF
9	Rothbury Hunter Valley Chardonnay	1995	Rothbury
10	Rothbury Hunter Valley Semillon	1996	Rothbury
11	Blackwood Park Riesling	1995	Blackwood Park
12	Château Tahbilk Goulburn Cabernet Sauvignon	1993	Château Tahbilk
16	St Johanner Abtey Kabinett	1996	St Johann
17	Messzelátó Dûlô Tokaji	1988	Messzelátó Dûlô
20	Viña Azabache	1996	Azabache

Databases often have special **forms** which can be used to enter data. These look rather like paper forms, with boxes that can be filled in. The information in a database form is checked when it is entered in the boxes. For example, in the box which asks for a person's age, a form would only accept a number.

Reports are often used to print out the contents of a database. A report is a way of presenting selected parts of a database formatted in a table. It is possible for the user to **query** the database (ask it for information). This is achieved using a **query**, which is a simple program that extracts information from one or more tables in a database.

It is also possible to use databases for **sorting** records, which means arranging records in a particular order. For example a database of customers could be sorted by date of birth, or by alphabetical order.

There are several types of database. The two main types are the following:

○ A **flatfile** (or **flat-file** or **flat**) **database** is a database which stores data simply as items, without giving the data an internal structure. All of the information is often stored in one very large table, which means that the database may take longer to find information. Flatfile databases are simple to set up, but less efficient at finding information than relational databases are.

○ A **relational database** stores data in multiple tables, which are connected or linked together. Any one piece of information in a relational database can be related to any other piece of information in the database. This is probably the most common type of database.

Spreadsheet programs

spreadsheet program	**formula**
spreadsheet	**function**
workbook	**column heading**
row	**row label**
column	**active cell**
cell	**cell range**
numeric data	**edit**
text	**chart**

A **spreadsheet program** is an application which is used to display data and to perform calculations on it. The word 'spreadsheet' is also used to refer to the product created by this type of application – for example a table of information in words and figures, either on the screen, as a file, or as a printout.

The word **spreadsheet** can be used to describe:

O a single file of information in a spreadsheet program

O the printed product

O the program itself

*We've made up a **spreadsheet** of all the payments this month– it's on my computer.*

*I'll give you a **spreadsheet** showing the latest test results.*

*You can calculate averages using a **spreadsheet** like Excel.*

In Excel, one of the most popular spreadsheet programs, the files used are called **workbooks**. These consist of worksheets, or 'sheets', which are the electronic equivalent of large sheets of paper. (Other programs may use different terms.) The data is displayed in **rows** and **columns**, in a large table on the screen. The columns are usually labelled with letters of the alphabet (though sometimes with a number) at the top of the worksheet, and the rows are labelled with numbers

Dialogue

An administrative assistant asks her colleague for some help with a database program:

**admin.
assistant**: Cathy, I've got a problem here. I'm trying to enter this customer's data into this form, but I keep getting an error message.

colleague: That's strange. Let me see ... Oh, I understand. You have to enter the customer's initials in that field. It won't let you leave it blank.

**admin.
assistant**: OK, I see. I'll just type it in.

colleague: There ... it's accepted it.

**admin.
assistant**: So is that information all stored on the database now?

colleague: That's right. You can retrieve this customer's record whenever you want.

on the left. The grey areas at the top of columns are called 'column headings', and the corresponding areas to the left of the rows are called 'row headings'. **Cells** are the small boxes formed where rows and columns intersect. Every cell has an 'address', which contains the labels of the row and column which intersect to form it, for example D5, shown here in Microsoft Excel.

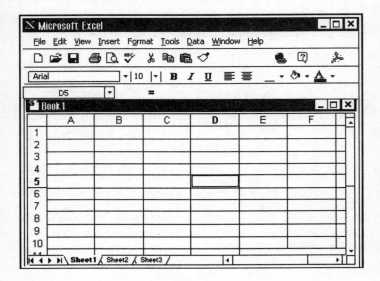

Cells can contain **numeric data**, **text**, **formulas** or **functions**. Text is used for titles, or to describe the figures being displayed. It is also often used to show worksheet headings, **column headings** and **row labels**. Numeric data can be entered using the keyboard or can result from calculations.

In order to enter data into a cell, the cell must be **active**. You can make a cell active by selecting it, either by clicking on the cell, or by moving the cursor to it using the up and down arrows on the keyboard and pressing 'enter' to select it. A continuous group of cells is called a **cell range**. For example the names shown in the screen below occupy the cell range A6–A10 (usually shown as A6:A10).

Formulas can be used in spreadsheet applications to perform calculations on the numbers shown in the worksheet. These can be used for relatively simple calculations, such as adding all the figures in a column, or they can perform more complex statistical calculations. For example, in the spreadsheet above, a formula could be used to work out the average number of units sold.

Functions are pre-prepared formulas, procedures or routines that perform a particular task. These are available in the program. The user can click on the function which he or she wants to use, instead of having to enter a long and complicated formula.

> Some common expressions relating to spreadsheet programs:
>
> **create** a spreadsheet
>
> **create** a chart
>
> **enter** data **into** a spreadsheet
>
> **extract** data **from** a spreadsheet
>
> **make** a cell active
>
> **perform** a calculation
>
> **work out** an average
>
> **carry out** or **execute** a function

It is easy to **edit** the data which has been entered into a worksheet. You can delete the contents of a cell by selecting it and pressing the 'delete' key on the keyboard. It is also possible to replace the contents of a cell by selecting it and typing or pasting in the new contents. You can also change the width of a column by clicking on its right-hand edge and dragging it to the left or right.

Charts can be created using a spreadsheet program. There are several types of chart – for example bar charts, line graphs, pie charts and scatter diagrams. The screenshot below shows examples of the different types of chart available in Excel.

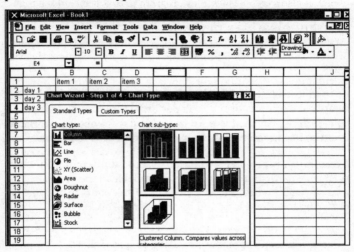

Other applications

personal information manager (PIM)	**web browser**
	Telnet
fax	**FTP client**
e-mail	**news client**
voice mail	

There is an unlimited range of possible applications software, as programs can be written for any professional or personal computing need. A few common examples are mentioned here:

Accounting and financial packages

There are specialized accounting packages used for keeping company and personal accounts. **Personal finance managers** are simple accounting programs for domestic use.

PIMs (personal information managers)

These are applications used by individuals for organizing everyday personal information such as lists of things to do, personal appointments, phone numbers etc. They may also include useful features such as a calendar. An example of this type of program is Microsoft Outlook, which is also a communications program in that it includes e-mail.

Communications packages

Many applications enable communication of various types. Below is a list of the main types of communications software currently available.

○ **fax**: As an alternative to the traditional fax machine, it is possible to send and receive faxes via a computer.

○ **e-mail**: a type of communications software that enables computer users to send typed messages to each other, using local networks, telephone lines, and/or the Internet; discussed in detail in Chapter 10.

○ **voice mail**: like a computer-based telephone answering machine, this is a feature of e-mail software which can support audio. This means that that users can leave each other spoken telephone messages which can be heard using the computer.

○ **web browser**: a program designed for navigating the World Wide Web, and for viewing, printing and saving web pages, or pages on intranet sites.

○ **Telnet**: an application used to log on to (and use) a remote computer.

○ **FTP client**: software used for transferring files from one computer to another via a network.

○ **news client**: a program used to read messages in, and send messages to, Usenet newsgroups. Modern browsers are capable of doing this too.

For more details on the last four points, see Chapter 9.

Buying and installing software

software bundle
software suite
software licence
pirate software
version
beta version
prerelease version
upgrade (noun)

upgrade (verb)
install
installation disk/CD
 ROM
Setup Wizard
typical installation
full installation
custom installation

When people buy a new computer, they often receive **software bundles**. These are software programs which are included in the price of the hardware bought by the customer. A **software suite** is a collection of applications which have been designed to work well together, for example Microsoft Office. Unless a program is freeware, or comes bundled with a computer, people have to pay to use it. The permission to use a program after payment is called a **software licence**. Illegal software is software which is not licensed. **Pirate software** is software which has been illegally copied, allowing people to avoid paying for licences.

software, program, package, application:

These words have very similar meanings, and are often used interchangeably. Notice, however, that software strictly includes text, graphics, audio, video or data files. These are not programs themselves, but are created, played or displayed by programs.

Note that **software** is an uncountable noun. It is **not** correct to say 'a software':

I'm going to buy some new software at the weekend.

It's quite easy to get free software on the Internet.

What software came bundled on your new computer?

I hope there isn't any illegal software on the system – Head Office are very strict about it.

Companies that produce applications try to develop new and improved **versions**. A version that is in the final stages of testing is called a **beta** or **prerelease version**. Customers who already own an earlier version do not usually have to pay full price for a new version. Instead, they buy an **upgrade**. When they install the upgrade, a special program **upgrades** the application, by updating the areas that have changed, and adding new features.

There are various ways of introducing, or **installing** software. Special floppies called **installation disks** are inserted one by one in order. Increasingly, **CD ROMS** are used, or the required files are downloaded from the Internet. In all cases it is common for the disks to run a program called a **Setup Wizard**, which gives the user step-by-step options. In many cases the user can choose between:

O a **typical installation**: the standard default version of the program.

O a **full installation**: a version of the program including all the extra features available.

O a **custom installation**: allows the user to choose the option he or she would like to include. An example of this might be Word, which can be installed with optional features such as Clip Art, Office Assistant or Help Files.

7

Programming and programming languages

> programmer   code
> programming language

Computers cannot function without programs, which give them instructions. People specialized in writing programs are known as computer **programmers**. They construct programs using **programming languages**. These are not spoken languages like French or Chinese, but are specified sets of words, phrases and symbols, called **code**, which can be combined in certain very restricted ways to instruct the computer. This is a complex and specialized area, and the following is not a comprehensive guide but a brief description of some of the most commonly used languages.

In instructing computers, three types of language can be identified – mark-up languages, scripting languages, and programming languages.

Mark-up languages

> mark-up language   XML (extensible mark-up
> mark up   language)
> HTML (hypertext mark-up   SGML (standard generalized
>   language)   mark-up language)

Mark-up languages are not actually programming languages. They do not create programs, but use code to **mark up**, or identify, elements of a text or data file. This allows the file to be displayed or printed in particular ways when it is opened in an application such as a word processor or a web browser. For example, the piece of mark-up language, or 'tag', '<b>' keyed in before a word or character indicates that a section of text should be shown in bold.

○ **HTML (hypertext mark-up language)**: the simplest mark-up language, used to create web and intranet pages.

○ **XML (extensible mark-up language)**: extends and builds on HTML; it is essentially a simplified version of SGML that is designed especially for marking up web and intranet documents.

○ **SGML (standard generalized mark-up language)**: widely used in publishing and research; it is a complex and comprehensive system that specifies rules for organizing and marking up (or 'tagging') elements of documents.

Scripting languages

scripting language	**Perl or PERL (practical**
script	**extraction and report**
JavaScript	**language)**

Scripting languages are languages used to write **scripts**, which are simple programs. They are often used on web and intranet pages. Two examples of scripting languages are:

○ **JavaScript**: often used to carry out simple tasks such as checking that the user has filled in all the required fields of a form on the Web before clicking on the 'submit' button.

○ **Perl** or **PERL (practical extraction and report language)**: probably the most commonly-used scripting language. It is often used on the Web for processing text input, in tasks such as checking online tests and sending the results to the students.

Programming languages

BASIC (beginners' all-purpose symbolic instruction code)	**LISP (list processing)**
	Delphi
	C
COBOL (common business oriented language)	**C++**
	bug
FORTRAN (formula translation)	**debug**
	debugger
Pascal	
ALGOL (algorithmic language)	

Scripts are relatively simple programs. However, more complex programs require more powerful languages. There is a huge variety of programming languages. The following are some of the best known and most commonly used.

- **BASIC (beginners' all-purpose symbolic instruction code)**: a relatively simple language. The more powerful, modernized version of this language is **VisualBasic** or **VB**, often used for creating programs that integrate and automate routines in Windows applications.

- **COBOL** (pronounced /'koʊbɒl/; **common business oriented language**): used in business mainly to write commercial applications. An example of its use is in accountancy applications. Although thought by some to be old and bulky, it is still said to be the most widely-used programming language in the world.

- **FORTRAN** (pronounced /'fɔːtran/; **formula translation**): designed to be used by scientists and engineers. It includes extensive mathematical and statistical capabilities, and was the first high-level programming language.

- **Pascal** (pronounced /pas'kɑːl/): often used to teach programming; its relative inflexibility has prevented it from becoming popular outside academic circles.

- **ALGOL** (pronounced /'algɒl/; **algorithmic language**): used mainly by mathematicians and scientists.

- **LISP** (pronounced /lɪsp/; **list processing**): used in research into artificial intelligence.

- **Delphi** (pronounced /'dɛlfɪ/): used in many applications, particularly in databases; it enables developers to quickly develop applications.

- **C and C++** (pronounced /'siː plʌs 'plʌs/): widely used high-level languages.

- **Java** (pronounced /'dʒɑːvə/): a powerful high-level language which is similar to C++. It was designed mainly to be used on the Web and on intranets.

Some common expressions relating to computer programming:

program a computer — to create and install a program which will run on it:
You can program the computer to perform that operation automatically.

write a program — to construct a program using a programming language:
*The course teaches you how to **write** simple **programs**.*

program in a language — to use a particular programming language:
*Can you **program in** C++?*

code or **do coding** — to write programs or scripts:
*I'm **doing some coding** for that new program.*

code up — to construct part of a program using a programming language:
I've coded up that form you asked for.

mark up a file — to identify and mark elements of a file using a mark-up language:
*He **marked up** elements of the file to be displayed in bold, using HTML.*

debug a program — to re-write sections which contain problems, or **bugs**:
*We've got a programmer coming to the office to **debug** the accounts program.*

debugger — a program which tests code for bugs:
*We've bought a **debugger** to test for bugs in the accounts program.*

Other programming terms

> **high-level language** **machine code**
> **low-level language** **source code**

○ **High-level languages** are close to human natural languages, and the commands sound similar to phrases, for example 'draw map'.

○ **Low-level languages** are closer to **machine code** – the basic instructions, expressed in ones and zeros, which the computer understands.

A distinction can be made between **source code** – the code entered by the programmer – and machine code – the basic code understood by the computer. All programs need to be translated into machine code by a special program, either before running or while running.

8

Networks, platforms and protocols

This chapter looks at how computers are connected together in networks.

> **stand-alone machine** **Internet**
> **network** **intranet**
> **LAN (local area** **authorization**
>   **network)** **firewall**
> **MAN (metropolitan** **extranet**
>   **area network)**
> **WAN (wide area**
>   **network)**

Although many individual computer users may have **stand-alone machines** (machines which are not connected to other computers), in institutional settings it is very common for two or more computers to be linked in a **network**. There are several types of network. Some of the most common are:

○ **LAN** or **local area network**: a network which covers a small physical area, for example one building. LANs allow users to have common access to data and equipment such as printers, in addition to being able to communicate with each other using e-mail.

○ **MAN** or **metropolitan area network**: a network which covers, for example, a city; may be used in contexts such as education.

○ **WAN** or **wide area network**: a network which covers an even wider area, in which machines are usually connected via telephone lines or radio. A WAN can be as small as two LANs which are connected, or as big as the **Internet** – the ultimate wide area network, covering the whole planet (see chapter 9 for more details on the Internet).

Dialogue

A new employee and her colleague are discussing a problem:

new employee: That's strange.

colleague: What's wrong?

new employee: I can't find that spreadsheet I was working on yesterday. I know I saved it.

colleague: Did you save it on your space on the server?

new employee: What do you mean?

colleague: Did you save it on the H drive? That's the shared storage area on the server. If you did, you should be able to open the file from any machine in the building – they're all linked up to a network.

new employee: Actually I think I might have saved it on the C drive, in the other office.

colleague: That means you saved it on the hard disk of that particular machine, so you won't be able to open the file on the machine you're using at the moment.

new employee: Oh, right. So will I have to go all the way upstairs to the fifth floor to get my spreadsheet?

colleague: I'm afraid so.

new employee: I'll make sure I store it on the server next time!

○ **intranet**: a network which uses the same technology as the Internet. The difference is that an intranet is private, and can only be accessed by a particular group of people, who have **authorization** (permission) to use it. An intranet is often protected from outsiders with a **firewall**, a system which makes the intranet secure. Intranets are often used in business and educational contexts. They may cover a geographically small area, or may be available to users over a large territory, and may even be global.

○ **extranet**: a network which lies between an intranet and the Internet. It is like an intranet, in the sense that it is a private network, but it allows different degrees of access to different groups or individuals, using passwords. For example, a company may have an intranet which their own employees can access fully, but which their business partners can only access partially. The parts that these authorized outsiders can access constitute the extranet.

Dialogue

A member of staff is showing a new employee the company's intranet:

staff member: This is the home page of our intranet on the screen now.

new employee: Oh, do you mean our web page, where our customers can find information about us using the Internet?

staff member: Well, no. This is something different. It's a page you view in your browser, but it's not on the World Wide Web. It's on an internal system called an intranet. It's a bit like a 'mini' Internet for the company.

new employee: I see. So what's it used for?

staff member: Mostly internal information, notices about special events, that kind of thing. It's really useful.

new employee: So can our customers see it too?

staff member: No, it's got a system called a firewall round it, which stops the outside world from accessing it.

Network topology

> **network topology** **ring topology**
> **bus topology** **star topology**

Networks can be arranged in different geometric patterns. This arrangement is called **network topology**. Three common topologies are:

○ **bus topology**: an arrangement of computer systems in a straight line, connected to a central cable, known as a **bus**; a bus network is cheap and easy to install, and is best suited to small networks.

○ **ring topology**: a circular arrangement; ring networks are more expensive and difficult to set up, but they can cover large distances.

○ **star topology**: an arrangement in a star shape, connected in the centre; star networks are fairly easy to install, but there can be problems when there is a lot of traffic passing through the central connection.

Network architecture

> **client–server architecture** **peer-to-peer architecture**
> **server** **fat client**
> **client** **thin client**

Within a network, computers may be set up in two different ways, or according to two different network architectures:

○ A **client–server architecture** is a design in which a powerful computer, called a **server**, provides information and/or applications software to other computers in a network. These other computers are called **clients**.

In a client–server relationship, the client may be described as a **fat client** or a **thin client**. A fat client is a client which has the capacity for performing its own data processing, although the data itself may be stored on the server. A thin client, in contrast, is a client which has very little processing power, relying mainly on the server for both data storage and processing.

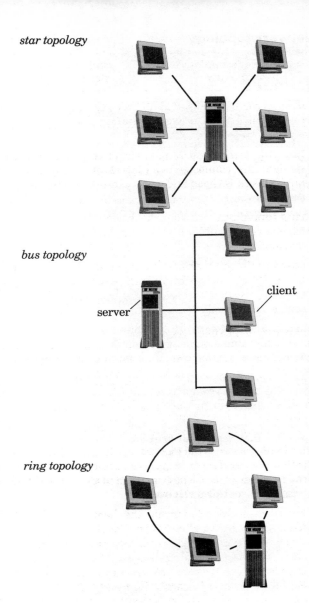

star topology

bus topology

server

client

ring topology

○ A **peer-to-peer architecture** is one in which all the computers have the same capabilities.

Platforms

platform	cross-platform

Platform is a term which refers to either a system's hardware, or its operating system, or a combination of the two. An example might be an Intel processor running Windows 95. The platform being used determines the type of applications which can be run on the system, although some programs and devices can be **cross-platform**, meaning that they can operate on more than one platform.

Network protocols

protocol	TCP/IP (transmission control protocol/Internet protocol)

Networks transmit data using different **protocols**. A protocol is a set of rules and signals which determine the way in which computers on a network communicate with each other.

The type of protocol used by a network decides, for example, the way in which data is compressed, and the rate at which it is transferred. A popular example of a protocol for LANs is Ethernet.

The Internet uses a 'suite' (collection) of protocols referred to as **TCP/IP**, which stands for **transmission control protocol/Internet protocol** – the two main protocols used in the suite. TCP/IP is the standard set of protocols used for transmitting data on the Internet, and is widely supported by network operating systems that use their own protocols.

9

The Internet and the World Wide Web

Expressions such as **information superhighway**, **cyberspace** and **surfing the Net** all refer to the most important and exciting development in modern computing – the growth of the **Internet** and the **World Wide Web**.

The **Net** (the Internet) and the **Web** (the World Wide Web) can be used for a variety of purposes by users worldwide. This section looks at the terms used to describe the range of functions performed by this technology, the equipment and software you need to get started, and the key words and phrases you will need to be able to talk about the Internet confidently in English.

What is the Internet?

cyberspace	newsgroup
the information superhighway	chat room
	online forum
electronic mail (e-mail)	

The Internet can be understood in various ways, reflecting its different aspects.

○ **a network of computers**

The Internet is the world's biggest network, linking every continent. People who meet on the Net are said to meet in **cyberspace** – a non-physical 'space' created by computer systems.

○ **an information resource**

The Internet contains information on an enormous range of topics of interest, and huge amounts of data are constantly being transferred between computers on the Internet. For this reason it is sometimes called the **information superhighway**, especially in the media. The World Wide Web is the main source of information on the Net, but you can also get information from other sources, which are described later in this chapter.

○ **a collection of services**

Many services, such as the World Wide Web, FTP, e-mail and Usenet run on the Internet, using different protocols (see chapter 8).

○ **a communication system**

The Internet links users all over the world using fast and relatively cheap forms of communication. **Electronic mail** (or, more commonly, **e-mail**) is the most widely-used service on the Internet, but people also use other forms of communication on the Internet such as **newsgroups**, **chat rooms** and **online forums** (explained later in this chapter).

○ **a community of users**

The Internet can be understood as a kind of community of people all over the world. People often make friends on the Net with people in distant countries, and there are thousands of special interest groups whose members use the Internet to keep in touch with each other.

Getting connected to the Internet

online services	direct network
ISP (Internet Service	connection
Provider)	cable modem
IAP (Internet Access	leased line
Provider)	web browser
modem	bandwidth
dial-up connection	bps (bits per second)
online	traffic
ISDN (Integrated	
Services Digital	
Network)	

There are various ways for users to get connected to the Internet.

You can get access to the Net using an **online service**, for example CompuServe or AOL (America Online), or through an **ISP** (an

Internet Service Provider), or an **IAP** (an **Internet Access Provider**). These are companies with large computers, which are permanently connected to the Net. Users usually pay to connect their computers to these computers (although increasingly this service is free), and may be connected in several ways:

○ A piece of equipment called a **modem** may be used, which translates the information used by the computer into information which can be sent by telephone. This information can then be transmitted through a **dial-up connection** on the telephone system, allowing the computer to communicate with other computers. This is the most common way of connecting to the Net for most domestic and commercial users. These users pay for the service in the same way that they pay for phone calls, as they are charged for the length of time they are **online** (using the Internet on a telephone line).

○ Another form of connection is **ISDN** (**Integrated Services Digital Network**), which uses special wires rather than normal telephone connections, and is capable of transmitting larger amounts of data more quickly than a standard dial-up connection.

○ If an Internet Service Provider is a company or university, the users are more likely to use a **direct network connection** instead of a modem and dial-up connection.

○ It is also possible to get connected via a **cable modem** – a modem which uses cable television lines and is much faster than a conventional modem and telephone line connection.

○ Yet another type of connection is via a **leased line**. This works like a dial-up connection but it is always active, and is charged at a fixed monthly rate.

○ Sometimes, radio, satellite or microwave connections are used.

In addition to a computer and its Internet connection, special programs are needed to use the Internet. A **web browser** (also known, technically, as a web client) is a type of program which allows users to view, download and print web pages. Examples of web browsers are Netscape Navigator and Internet Explorer.

You are **online**, or **on the Internet**, or **on the Net** when you have access to the Internet on your computer:

*Are you **on the Internet** yet?*

*I'll be **online** next week, so I'll be able to e-mail you.*

The amount of data which can be transferred within a certain length of time via an Internet connection is determined by **bandwidth**. Bandwidth is expressed in **bps**, which means **bits per second**. If it takes a long time for you to download material from the Internet, this may be because you, or the provider of the material, does not have enough bandwidth to deal efficiently with the amount of data being transferred. **Traffic** refers to the volume of data being transferred via a communications system. Traffic is said to be 'heavy' or 'light'.

The World Wide Web

the World Wide Web	**website**
hypertext	**hyperlink**
web page	

It is common for people to think that the **World Wide Web** is another name for the Internet, but really the Web is just one of the services that runs on the Internet. It is, however, the most well-known, and probably the most widely-used, information resource on the Internet. The Web is an enormous network of information in the form of **hypertext**, which is a way of organizing and linking pages of information in a flexible, non-linear way. Hypertext enables the user to move between different elements of **web pages**, or between different **websites** (see below) by means of **links** or **hyperlinks**. This makes finding information on the Web very quick and easy.

What is a web page?

website	**site map**
web page	**main menu**
HTML (HyperText	**front page**
Mark-up Language)	**splash page**
home page	

The information on the Web is displayed in **websites**, which can consist of one or many **web pages**. Web pages are different from word-processed documents, as they are written in a special programming language called **HTML – hypertext mark-up language** (see chapter 7 for more details).

There are several special terms used to talk about pages on the Internet. These words are used by different people to mean slightly different things, but generally they can be summarized as follows:

○ **home page**

The main page of a website is the home page, which is often connected to other pages in the site. A home page may contain or link to a **site map**, which is a graphic plan of the contents of the website. The site map may be shown as a diagram, for example in the form of a 'family tree'. Alternatively, the home page might show a list of contents, which is usually called the **main menu**. Note that people sometimes use the term 'home page' to refer to their own personal website.

Chambers Harrap home page

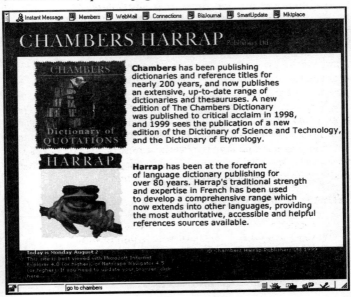

○ **front page**

This term is used to talk about the first page that an Internet user sees in a website, using the main website address. In practice, this is very often the home page – the main page of the site. A very decorative or colourful front page is sometimes called a **splash page**. FrontPage is also the name of a Microsoft program used for creating web pages.

Elements of web pages

background	hit counter
frame	page view
frameset	hit
pane	

○ The **background** is the colour or pattern which is seen 'behind' the text and other elements on the screen.

○ The page may be organized into sections, which the user may be able to scroll up and down separately. These sections are called **frames**, and a page showing several frames is technically called a **frameset**. (This contrasts with **panes**, which are areas of an application window that display different elements of the page.)

A **hit** is:

○ an instance of accessing a web page:

This page received over 300 hits yesterday.

○ a 'match' in search engine results (see page 80):

The search I did resulted in 350 hits, so I tried again with more specific keywords.

○ a request made of a web server:

Our web server received over 3000 hits yesterday.

You **hit** a key on the keyboard when you press it:

If you type the wrong word, select the relevant text and hit 'Delete'.

○ The **hit counter** is an element on a web page which is automatically updated to show the number of times that the page has been accessed. The hit counter records **page views** (instances of a user accessing the web page on which the counter appears). However, some reflect all hits to a site, that is, requests for any files on web pages. This gives a misleadingly high number.

Online forms

online form	**push button**
form field	**check box**
text box	**confirmation page**
radio button	

Many websites include **online forms** for users to fill in with information such as their home address, for example when they are ordering goods. The user enters the information in various **form fields** (categories of information). Forms typically have the following features:

○ **text boxes**: spaces for users to type in text.

○ **radio buttons**: small circular buttons with a dark dot in the centre (when selected), which users can click on.

○ **push buttons**: buttons with text which users can click on; these buttons often display the words 'submit', 'send', or 'reset' (or 'clear').

○ **check boxes**: small boxes which the user clicks on to enter a check mark, or a 'tick' (✓).

○ **confirmation page**: a page automatically displayed when a user successfully submits information via an online form.

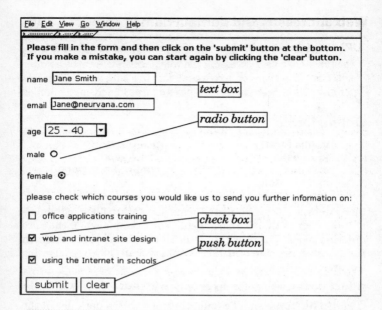

Many words related to the Internet have variable spellings. Certain words are variously written as one word, two words with a hyphen, or two separate words. In addition, initial capital letters are sometimes used, and sometimes not.

Examples

Website; Web-site; Web site

website; web-site; web site.

A similar variation can be seen with **e-mail**, **home page** and **online**. There are no 'correct' versions of these words, but generally, the use of lower case (non-capitals) is more informal; putting two words together can also appear more and modern. It is best to use the same style within a text, and the same style as other people in the context in which you are communicating, if you are unsure.

Web addresses and domain names

> URL (Uniform Resource Locator)
> web address
> domain name
> path
>
> IP (Internet Protocol) address
> DNS, (Domain Name System)
> case sensitive

Every website (and every file on a site) has its own address, made up of a sequence of characters in a particular order. This address is known as a **URL** (**Uniform Resource Locator**), although non-specialists very often refer to URLs simply as **web addresses**.

The **domain name** is the part of the URL which identifies the company or organization, type of organization (eg. educational or commercial), and often the country (if it is not a US domain name). An example of a domain name is:

chambersharrap.co.uk

A section that appears after the domain name, before the file name of a particular web page, is known as the **path**, as it shows the route to the file.

Computers use **IP** (**Internet Protocol**) **addresses** to identify machines. IP addresses consist of numbers and dots, for example:

195.89.148.137

These addresses are difficult for people to remember easily, however, so we usually use memorable domain names like the one above (chambersharrap.co.uk). **DNS** (**Domain Name System**) enables servers to translate a memorable domain name into an IP address.

File names and directories on web servers can be **case sensitive**, which means you must type them using **UPPER CASE** or **lower case** correctly. If you make a mistake with the case in an address, it may not be recognized.

Finding information on the World Wide Web

location box	navigate
search engine	guest
database	forward/back buttons
keyword	directories
Boolean operators	categories
results	Edit menu
results page	Find in Page
visit	surf

If you know exactly what you are looking for, and you already know the address of a web page, you can open up your browser, and type the address into the space called the **location box** (or 'address box', 'location field' or 'address field') – see page 83 – near the top of the screen. You then press 'Enter' on your keyboard. Your program will then take you to that page.

However, you may want to look up a particular topic, or just have a general look around an area, rather than look for a specific site.

Probably the easiest way to look for information on the Web is to use a **search engine**. A search engine is a facility which works by building up a huge **database** of information extracted from websites, enabling you to find information by searching for **keywords**, which you type in. When entering keywords, you can use the words AND, OR or NOT to clarify your search. These words used in this context are called **Boolean operators**. Some well known search engines are Alta Vista, Excite and Lycos.

Search engines present you with the **results** of a search in the form of a list of links on a new page called a **results page**, with the sites which contain most examples of the keyword or keywords nearer the top. You can then click on the links of the sites or pages you would like to **visit**.

Directories are similar to search engines, but have **categories** within which you can search, for example education, or sport. Yahoo! is a popular directory. It is also possible to use a search facility to look for information within a web page, using the **Edit menu** of the browser. In that menu you can click on **Find in Page** and enter a keyword.

> Someone who likes **surfing the Web**, or **surfing the Net**, likes looking at web pages and moving between different sites, without necessarily having a particular target in mind:
>
> *'How do you find things on the Web?'*
>
> *'Well, sometimes I just **surf** until I find something interesting.'*

Common features of web browsers

drop-down menu	hot spot
status bar	image map
toolbar	graphic
location box	pointing hand
bookmark	navigation bar (nav bar)
favorites	forward/back button
navigate	Go menu
link/hyperlink	History

A browser programme is used for reading web pages. It has several features which are similar to many other programs, for example **drop-down menus** and **toolbars**. These features are all discussed in detail in chapter 4.

The **location box** is usually found near the top of the browser window, below the main tool bar. It is the place where the URLs, or web addresses, can be seen or entered.

You can mark websites by using **bookmarks**, or **favorites** in your browser. This facility allows you to make a personalized collection of the addresses of sites you visit frequently. You can access these directly by going into a special menu, instead of having to type in the addresses again.

When talking about the World Wide Web, people often use words which normally indicate physical movement, reflecting the fact that the Internet is seen as a type of 'space'.

visit a website:

Why not visit our website, to find out more about our wide range of products?

navigate between pages:

A well-structured website enables users to navigate easily between pages.

go to a page:

To order any product, please go to the sales page.

return to a page:

Click on the company logo on any page of the site to return to the home page.

explore the Web:

You may like to explore the Web for more information on this topic.

There are also elements on the screen which suggest this:

forward/back buttons:

Click on the back button in your browser to go to the page you were on before.

home page:

You can click on this link to go back to the site's home page.

Microsoft use the term **bookmark** for points within pages that are the targets of links.

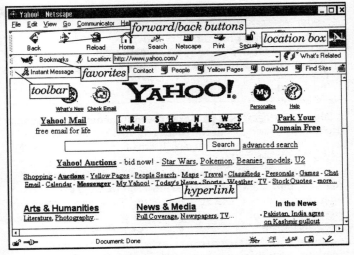

Moving around, or **navigating** between, or within, pages on a website, or between websites is easy, because pages are linked. These **links** (or **hyperlinks**) usually appear as blue <u>underlined text</u>. Links to other pages can also appear as **hot spots** – areas of the page which react to a mouse click. For example, you may find a hot spot on an **image map**. This is a picture, or **graphic**, with different parts which link to different targets if you click on them. You usually know you have found a hot spot when your mouse pointer changes from an arrow to **a pointing hand**. If you want to follow a link, you click on it with the mouse, and it will take you to a new page. The **navigation bar**, or '**nav bar**' is an area along the edge of a page, that displays links to the main parts of the site, which you can click on.

You can also use the **forward** and **back buttons** to move around on the Web, retracing your steps on the route that you have already taken. Alternatively, you can go into the **Go** (or **History**) **menu**, which will show you the last few sites you have visited. You can then click on the site that you want to return to. It is also possible to save a web page, or part of it, such as a graphic, to disk.

Creating web pages

web-authoring programs   host
content creator   webmaster
information architecture   update
front end   launch
back end

In addition to browsing pages on the Web, many Net users are becoming increasingly interested in creating their own pages. This used to be a rather specialized skill, involving the use of HTML (HyperText Mark-up Language), but now it is much easier, since programs like FrontPage have been developed. **Web-authoring** programs (also known as HTML editors) allow users to create web pages as easily as creating a document in a word-processing program. However, there are specialists who work in this area, helping organizations to create websites which are attractive and easy to use. **Content creators** or editors are the people in charge of deciding what information should be contained in the site. Other specialists may be in charge of the **information architecture**, which is the art of structuring a website to make access easy and logical for the users. Other web developers may be responsible for the general look and feel of the site, which is known as the **front end**, the part the user sees and interacts with. The **back end** refers to the server-side technical aspects of running a website, for example, integrating it with a database.

When a website is ready, it can be put on the Web. This is often done by paying a **host** company. A host company **hosts** web pages. This means that it provides the necessary hardware, software and connections from its servers to the Internet, while the actual content remains under the customer's control. The host company then charges a fee for publishing them on the World Wide Web. In a company, the person in charge of the web page is sometimes called the **webmaster**, although increasingly this responsibility is shared by a team of people. The webmaster is responsible for **updating** the website – adding new information to keep it up to date. When a new site is introduced to the Web, we can say that it is **launched**.

Other services on the Internet

FTP (File Transfer Protocol)
Usenet
newsgroup/online forum
threads
Telnet
IRC (Internet Relay Chat)
chat room

BBS (Bulletin Board System)
specialized search engine
FTP search engine
newsgroup search engine
download
upload
post

In addition to web browsers, other types of program and service may be used to access different services on the Net, for example:

○ **FTP (File Transfer Protocol)** clients are used to transfer large files or sets of files. Many FTP servers require a user name and password, but others, known as 'anonymous FTP servers', are open to non-registered users.

○ **Usenet** is a service that is used to access **newsgroups** (or **online forums**). These are online discussion groups on specialized fields of interest. Newsgroups show messages organized into **threads**, which are chains of messages and replies ordered in sequence, so users can 'follow the thread' of an e-mail discussion.

○ **Telnet** is a program that allows you to access and use a distant computer.

○ **IRC (Internet Relay Chat)** is a service which allows people to communicate via the Internet in real time (in virtual areas called '**chat rooms**'), by typing messages on to the screen, which the receiver can see a moment later.

○ A **BBS (Bulletin Board System)** allows people using the Internet to leave electronic messages on virtual 'notice boards', and also to read messages from other people.

○ **Specialized search engines** can be used to look for information on the Internet. An **FTP search engine** can be used to search for information on FTP servers. You can also find information in newsgroups by using Deja.com, which has a **newsgroup search engine**.

download a file	to take a file from another location, eg. a web server, and save it on a computer:
	You can download the software from our website.
upload a file	to transfer a file from a computer to a another location, eg. a web server:
	You can publish your web pages by uploading them to the web server.
post a message	to place a message on a bulletin board, or send it to a newsgroup:
	If you want to find out more about phrasal verbs, you should post a message to the alt.usage.english newsgroup.

Privacy and security on the Internet

hacker	netiquette
firewall	snail mail
encryption	troll (verb)
decrypt	troll (noun)
PGP (pretty good privacy)	newbie
flame (verb)	lurk
flame (noun)	spam

Because the Internet is not owned or run by one company or organization, it is not strictly regulated. While this may make the Internet more interesting and varied, it also means that users can be vulnerable to unwanted attention or even harassment by other users.

People and organizations may also want to protect private or sensitive data from those who deliberately enter into areas without authorization. These people are often called **hackers**, a term which was originally used simply to talk about computer enthusiasts, particularly self-taught programmers. The word has increasingly come to be used in the negative sense described above.

Organizations and individual Internet users can protect themselves from 'hackers', using a device called a **firewall**. This is a system which prevents people from gaining unauthorized access to private networks or machines.

Another way of increasing security when sending data on the Internet is to use **encryption**. This a kind of translation of ordinary data into secret code, which can be decoded, or **'decrypted'** only by the people it is intended for, who use a special software 'key' to decipher the encrypted data. An example of **encryption software** is **PGP**, which means '**pretty good privacy**'.

E-commerce

e-commerce	**shopping cart**
electronic commerce	**digital cash**

E-commerce or **electronic commerce** is commercial activity which takes place online. For example, Internet users can buy things online using a **shopping cart**, which is a piece of software used for ordering goods. They can pay for goods and services using credit cards, or can use **digital cash**.

Digital cash is a type of 'virtual money'. Each dollar has a serial number, and is anonymous, like real cash, and so does not show any information about the sender, unlike credit card numbers.

FAQs (Frequently Asked Questions)

FAQ (Frequently Asked Questions)	**ad click**
	time-out
mirror site	
banner ad	
click-through	

A familiar feature of many websites is the **FAQ** (pronounced /fak/) section. This is an area which shows the questions which users most often ask (the 'frequently asked questions') about the topic covered by the site, with answers. Newsgroups nearly always have a FAQ, and it strongly recommended that new subscribers check to see whether their query is covered in the FAQ before they post a question to the group. Here is an example of a FAQ file from an Internet enthusiasts' website, showing a few more points related to Internet terminology.

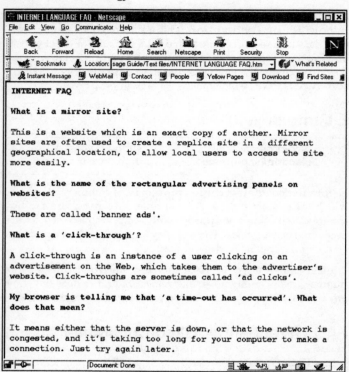

Below are some words and expressions that are most commonly used by very regular Net users:

flame (someone) (*verb*): to send a highly critical message to somebody in *eg.* a newsgroup:

I asked a stupid question, and about 50 people flamed me.

flame (*noun*): a highly critical message sent to someone in a newsgroup:

If you don't understand how newsgroups work, you can easily make a mistake, and receive flames from other subscribers.

netiquette: 'etiquette', or acceptable behaviour, of Net users:

It's important to observe netiquette if you want to avoid being flamed.

snail mail: the traditional postal system:

Attached are some notes about the current project. I've sent the other documents back to you by snail mail.

troll (*verb*): to deliberately provoke flames, or try to attract ignorant responses from new Net users, for fun:

He can't be serious; he must be trolling.

troll (*noun*): an instance of deliberately provoking flames:

That post must be a troll; no-one can be that stupid.

newbie: a new user on the Internet or a new subscriber of a newsgroup:

He must be a newbie – no-one else would ask a simple question like that.

spam: electronic mail, usually advertising products or services, sent to e-mail users, even though they haven't requested it:

Inform your I.T. manager if you get any spam, and they'll filter it out for you.

lurk: to read messages sent to a newsgroup, without sending any yourself:

It's a good idea to lurk for a while before you post your first message.

10

E-mail

Electronic mail, or **e-mail** is the most commonly-used service on the Internet, with the volume of traffic increasing every year as more and more people start using it.

Note the various ways of spelling **e-mail** (*noun*):

e-mail, **email**, **Email**, or **E-mail**.

The most common forms are **e-mail** and **email**. In this book we use the form with lower case 'e' and a hyphen (**e-mail**).

The verb is usually spelt **e-mail** or **email**:

*I'll **e-mail** you tomorrow with the details.*

*She says she **e-mailed** me, but I didn't receive anything.*

*They're **e-mailing** their friends in the States.*

*He **emails** me every day.*

*I **emailed** him with the answer.*

*I'm just **emailing** Jenny the dates for the conference.*

Note that you can:

e-mail someone: *I e-mailed Jenny.*

e-mail someone with information: *I e-mailed her with the dates.*

e-mail someone information: *I e-mailed her the dates.*

E-mail is pronounced 'ee' mail: /'iː meɪl/

E-mail is an increasingly common means of communication world-wide, and is becoming a popular alternative to faxes, telephone calls and conventional mail. It is very quick, cheap and easy to use, and it is also extremely convenient. You do not need paper or stamps,

and you can store messages you send and receive without taking
up any physical space.

Getting connected

e-mail address	web-based account
identifier	Internet café
mailbox	e-mail account
domain name	download
case sensitive	e-mail program
server-based account	

E-mail is a service which runs on the Internet, so users must have
access to the Internet to be able to use it. Internet Service Providers
(ISPs) supply customers with an e-mail address, and advise them
on how to set up their e-mail clients and/or browsers to send and
receive mail.

An **e-mail address** contains an **identifier**, which can be your
real name, or a nickname if you prefer. This appears in the first
part of the address, and enables the computer receiving the mail
to identify the associated user name (if this is different), and store
the mail in the user's **mailbox**. After the user name comes the @
('at') symbol. The next part of the address shows the **domain
name**. This identifies the server which is used to send and receive
your mail. The domain name shows the name and type of organization (for example educational, or commercial), and country code,
if it is not a United States domain name (see Appendix A). These
elements of the domain name are separated by dots.

Mary.Jones@ed.ac.uk

Mary.Jones	@	ed	.ac	.uk
identifier (user name or alias)	'at' symbol	name of organization	type of organization	country

E-mail addresses must be entered correctly, and user names may
be **case sensitive** (that is, it may be necessary to use capital or
lower case letters in parts of the name). There are no spaces between

92

the characters, and there is no full stop or dot at the end. Special characters or symbols (such as dollar signs, quotation marks or apostrophes) are not allowed.

Mary.Jones@ed.ac.uk

is pronounced

'Mary dot Jones, at E D, dot A C, dot U K'

/i: 'di: dɒt eɪ 'si: dɒt ju: 'keɪ/

or

'Mary dot Jones, at 'ed, dot ack, dot U K'

/'ɛd dɒt 'ak dɒt ju: 'keɪ/

There are two main types of e-mail account – either **server-based**, which is usual in institutions such as universities and large companies, and for anyone who subscribes with an ISP, or **web-based**, which can be accessed from any online computer. This type of account can be used in an **Internet café** – a special type of coffee shop where you can pay to access the Internet. People need your e-mail address in order to be able to send messages to your **e-mail account**, where they are stored in your mailbox until you **download** and read them with your **e-mail program** (also known as an e-mail client) or browser. Examples of popular e-mail programs are Pegasus Mail, Eudora Pro and Microsoft Outlook.

---

check your e-mail   to look to see if you have any new mail:
'Are you going to be using that computer for much longer?'
'No, I won't be long, I'm just checking my e-mail.'

Sending an e-mail

new message	**address book**
Cc (carbon copy)	**e-mail attachment**
Bcc (blind carbon copy)	

In order to compose an e-mail, you need to select the e-mail software's icon or File menu option for creating a **new message**. A message window opens, made up of a series of 'fields' (areas) into which is typed the destination address (or addresses), a heading or subject, and the text of the message.

Below is an example of a 'New Message' window from a commonly-used e-mailing program (Netscape Messenger).

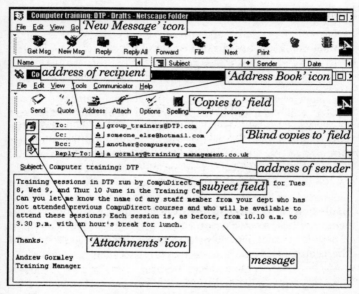

The **Cc** (**carbon copy**) field and **Bcc** (**blind carbon copy**) field are used for sending copies of the message to other people. The blind copy field is used to send a copy of the message to someone whose name the sender does not want to be shown on the message received by the other recipients.

If the sender types more than one destination address in the first box, the addresses are separated either by a comma or a semicolon, depending on the software being used. If using an electronic **address book**, the user can select 'multiple recipients' in the To field, the Cc field , and the Bcc field, simply by clicking on each name in turn.

Next to 'Subject', the sender writes the subject of the message. This helps both the sender and the recipient(s) to file the message so that it is easier to find and refer to later.

E-mail is useful not only for sending and receiving messages, but also for sending files using the Internet. When you send any kind of file via e-mail, it is called an **e-mail attachment**.

E-mail styles and conventions

The convenience of e-mail encourages a lot of people to communicate frequently, perhaps more often than they would using other means. As e-mail is used differently from other forms of written and spoken communication, it has developed its own styles and conventions.

E-mails are very often written in a different style from letters. They can be shorter and more informal, especially when they are written between friends and colleagues. However, the style you choose to adopt in e-mails depends very much on your relationship to the addressee (or recipient), the reason for e-mailing, and how often you are in contact with that person using e-mail.

E-mail greetings and endings

One area of difference is in greetings. In a letter, it is normal to start with a greeting like 'Dear Ms Black', or 'Dear Anne'. In an e-mail, it is also acceptable to begin in this way – but it is also very common to write only the person's name. If you want to be less formal you can begin with 'Hi Anne', 'Hi', or you can even use no greeting.

The same applies to the ending of an e-mail. In more formal e-mail messages, it is often a good idea to use the same kind of ending that you would use in a letter, especially when approaching someone for the first time. However, in informal messages between friends or colleagues, it is more common to use an informal ending, especially if you e-mail that person very often. Here is a summary of some of the ways people begin and end their messages.

Greetings	**Endings**
More formal	*More formal*
Dear Mr. Brown	Yours faithfully
Dear John	Yours sincerely
	Yours truly (especially in American English)
	Yours
	Regards
	Best wishes
Less formal	*Less formal*
John	Take care
Hi John	See you
Hi	See you later
(no greeting)	All the best
	(Only your name, eg. 'Peter')

It is also possible to add your own automatic **signature** (known as a **sig** for short) – a short personalized text file containing your name and contact details, which can be set to appear automatically at the bottom of all the messages you send.

Levels of formality

The degree of formality in e-mails is determined by the relationship between the writer and the recipient. Generally, more formal e-mails are similar to letters, less formal ones are similar to speech.

When writing an e-mail for the first time to someone you have never met, it is normal to use a relatively formal style, as you would for a formal letter. This style is also generally best used when writing to senior colleagues, or to officials.

formal e-mail

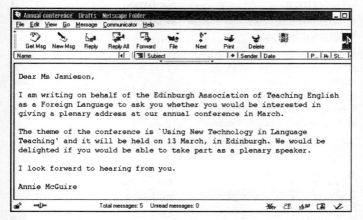

Dear Ms Jamieson,

I am writing on behalf of the Edinburgh Association of Teaching English as a Foreign Language to ask you whether you would be interested in giving a plenary address at our annual conference in March.

The theme of the conference is `Using New Technology in Language Teaching' and it will be held on 13 March, in Edinburgh. We would be delighted if you would be able to take part as a plenary speaker.

I look forward to hearing from you.

Annie McGuire

business e-mail

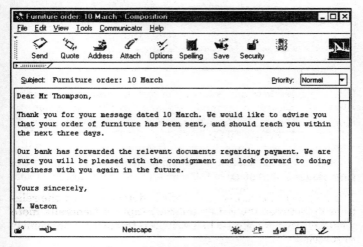

Subject: Furniture order: 10 March

Dear Mr Thompson,

Thank you for your message dated 10 March. We would like to advise you that your order of furniture has been sent, and should reach you within the next three days.

Our bank has forwarded the relevant documents regarding payment. We are sure you will be pleased with the consignment and look forward to doing business with you again in the future.

Yours sincerely,

M. Watson

If you are unsure about which style to use in an e-mail, and particularly if the message is important, it is best to use a more formal style, as it will generally not cause offence. If the person replies in a more informal style, you may follow that style in your next message.

This more formal type of e-mail is also common in business contexts, where e-mails are often retained for the company's records, and so may be regarded as an official and permanent record of communication, like a letter.

E-mail is a very flexible form of communication, and a wide variety of styles exists. In contrast to the formal message shown above, many e-mail messages are written in a less formal style. These more informal messages may be sent between friends, or colleagues who have a relaxed working relationship, perhaps colleagues around the same level in an organization.

Here is an example of a less formal message sent from one colleague to another.

less formal e-mail

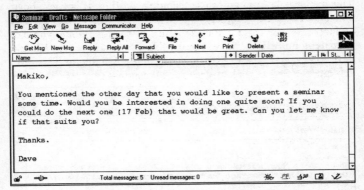

The language in this e-mail is more informal: for example '... that would be great', instead of 'we would be delighted if ...', and use of first names only instead of full names or title and surname. Note also that there is no formal ending as there is in the first example.

The most informal e-mails are generally sent between close friends. These messages are sometimes more similar to speech than to writing.

very informal e-mail

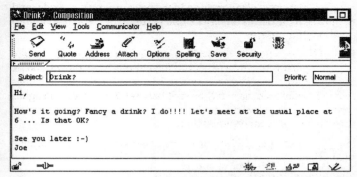

This message is from one close friend to another. It is very short, and uses speech-like language, for example 'How's it going?' instead of 'How are you?', and 'Fancy a drink?' instead of 'Would you like to go out for a drink?' The writer uses direct questions, which could be used in speech, either face to face or on the telephone. This kind of e-mail invites a quick and informal response.

Informal conventions

> **lower case**   **emoticon**
> **abbreviation**

Apart from general style, some very regular users of informal e-mail use certain conventions.

o Some people use all **lower case** (not capital letters) in informal messages, avoiding capitals, even in names.

for example:

i'm going to london to see john.

However, not everyone regards this as acceptable – it is best used with close friends, or others who also use that style.

o **Abbreviations** are sometimes used in informal messages.

99

Some abbreviations are:

AFAICT	as far as I can tell
AFAIK	as far as I know
AIUI	as I understand it
B4	before
BTW	by the way
cld	could
doc	document
EOF	end of file
FAQ	frequently asked questions
FOC	free of charge
foll	following *or* to follow
FWIW	for what it's worth
FYI	for your information
GR8	great
HTH	hope this helps
IIRC	if I recall correctly
IMHO	in my humble opinion
IMO	in my opinion
IOW	in other words
ISTM	it seems to me
ITRO	in the region of
NRN	no reply necessary
NW!	no way! *or* no!
msg	message
OTOH	on the other hand
OTT	over the top
PD	public domain
prhps	perhaps
TBD	to be discussed
TIA	thanks in advance
TNX	thanks
TVM	thanks very much
VR	virtual reality
WRT	with regard to

○ Some people use **emoticons** – small icons made up of punctuation characters. These are used to show the emotions or attitudes of the writer.

Some commonly used emoticons are:

:-)	'smiling'
:-(	'sad'
:-O	'bored' or 'surprised'
:-<	'frowning' or 'surprised'
;-)	'winking' ('I'm not entirely serious')

General conventions

○ You can use **right angle brackets** (>) in your e-mails to show text that another user has written, and to identify which messages you are responding to. Normally one angle bracket indicates that you are quoting text written by the person you are replying to. Two angle brackets >> indicate that you are quoting a second person, and so on.

○ In e-mails, it is not necessary to write your postal address at the top of a message as in letters, as it can be included in your 'signature' at the bottom. Similarly, people do not normally write the postal address of the person they are writing to in an e-mail message.

○ Generally, using ALL CAPITALS is regarded as the e-mail equivalent of shouting, and so should be used with care. There are other ways of emphasizing things more gently. For example you can use an asterisk *at the beginning and end of the part you want to stress*. Sometimes, people use underscore characters _before, and after_ the part of text they wish to stress.

Other functions of e-mail

address list	**low traffic**
mailing list	**high traffic**
digest version	

In your e-mail program you can create convenient **address lists** (or 'distribution lists'), and you can make up **mailing lists** kept in the electronic address book, which allow you to send the same message to a group of addresses in one operation. Special mailing lists with automated subscribing and unsubscribing are often created for members of 'special interest groups' to keep in touch with each other. They can be received in two ways – either as individual messages, or as a **digest version**, which collects all the messages and puts them in one e-mail, where you can click on the messages you want to read. If it is a **low traffic** list, with a low frequency of messages, you may receive the digest version every week or month. If it is a **high traffic** list, you may receive them more often, for example every week or every day.

Common problems

junk mail	virus
spam	virus checker
filtering	

One of the less enjoyable aspects of e-mail is **junk mail**, or '**spam**'. These terms refer to unwanted messages, normally sent automatically to multiple recipients, that are sometimes offensive in their content. You can take steps to avoid receiving spam, by **filtering** it out. You can instruct your e-mail program to take out messages containing particular elements.

Unfortunately computer users can also experience another type of problem – **viruses**. These are unwanted hidden programs which may destroy information stored on your computer and can sometimes spread through e-mail attachments. For this reason it is always a good idea to use a program called a **virus checker** first, before saving or opening an attachment you are unsure about. An example of this type of program is Dr Solomon's Anti Virus Toolkit.

Appendix A

Country codes for web and e-mail addresses

Below is a list of country identification codes that you may find in domain names (see page 92). Note that the suffix **.com** can be used by anyone, anywhere in the world, and is not restricted to companies within the United States.

AD Andorra
AE United Arab Emirates
AF Afghanistan
AG Antigua and Barbuda
AI Anguilla
AL Albania
AM Armenia
AN Netherlands Antilles
AO Angola
AQ Antarctica
AR Argentina
AS American Samoa
AT Austria
AU Australia
AW Aruba
AZ Azerbaijan

BA Bosnia and Herzegovina
BB Barbados
BD Bangladesh
BE Belgium
BF Burkina Faso
BG Bulgaria
BH Bahrain
BI Burundi
BJ Benin
BM Bermuda
BN Brunei Darussalam
BO Bolivia

BR Brazil
BS Bahamas
BT Bhutan
BV Bouvet Island
BW Botswana
BY Belarus
BZ Belize

CA Canada
CC Cocos (Keeling) Islands
CF Central African Republic
CG Congo
CH Switzerland
CI Cote D'Ivoire (Ivory Coast)
CK Cook Islands
CL Chile
CM Cameroon
CN China
CO Colombia
CR Costa Rica
CS Czechoslovakia (former)
CU Cuba
CV Cape Verde
CX Christmas Island
CY Cyprus
CZ Czech Republic

DE Germany
DJ Djibouti

DK Denmark
DM Dominica
DO Dominican Republic
DZ Algeria

EC Ecuador
EE Estonia
EG Egypt
EH Western Sahara
ER Eritrea
ES Spain
ET Ethiopia

FI Finland
FJ Fiji
FK Falkland Islands
 (Malvinas)
FM Micronesia
FO Faroe Islands
FR France
FX France, Metropolitan

GA Gabon
GB Great Britain (UK)
GD Grenada
GE Georgia
GF French Guiana
GH Ghana
GI Gibraltar
GL Greenland
GM Gambia
GN Guinea
GP Guadeloupe
GQ Equatorial Guinea
GR Greece
GS S. Georgia and S.
 Sandwich Isls.
GT Guatemala
GU Guam
GW Guinea-Bissau
GY Guyana

HK Hong Kong
HM Heard and McDonald
 Islands
HN Honduras
HR Croatia (Hrvatska)
HT Haiti
HU Hungary

ID Indonesia
IE Ireland
IL Israel
IN India
IO British Indian Ocean
 Territory
IQ Iraq
IR Iran
IS Iceland
IT Italy

JM Jamaica
JO Jordan
JP Japan

KE Kenya
KG Kyrgyzstan
KH Cambodia
KI Kiribati
KM Comoros
KN Saint Kitts and Nevis
KP Korea (North)
KR Korea (South)
KW Kuwait
KY Cayman Islands
KZ Kazakhstan

LA Laos
LB Lebanon
LC Saint Lucia
LI Liechtenstein
LK Sri Lanka
LR Liberia
LS Lesotho

LT Lithuania
LU Luxembourg
LV Latvia
LY Libya

MA Morocco
MC Monaco
MD Moldova
MG Madagascar
MH Marshall Islands
MK Macedonia
ML Mali
MM Myanmar
MN Mongolia
MO Macau
MP Northern Mariana Islands
MQ Martinique
MR Mauritania
MS Montserrat
MT Malta
MU Mauritius
MV Maldives
MW Malawi
MX Mexico
MY Malaysia
MZ Mozambique

NA Namibia
NC New Caledonia
NE Niger
NF Norfolk Island
NG Nigeria
NI Nicaragua
NL Netherlands
NO Norway
NP Nepal
NR Nauru
NT Neutral Zone
NU Niue
NZ New Zealand (Aotearoa)

OM Oman

PA Panama
PE Peru
PF French Polynesia
PG Papua New Guinea
PH Philippines
PK Pakistan
PL Poland
PM St. Pierre and Miquelon
PN Pitcairn
PR Puerto Rico
PT Portugal
PW Palau
PY Paraguay

QA Qatar

RE Reunion
RO Romania
RU Russian Federation
RW Rwanda

SA Saudi Arabia
Sb Solomon Islands
SC Seychelles
SD Sudan
SE Sweden
SG Singapore
SH St. Helena
SI Slovenia
SJ Svalbard and Jan Mayen
   Islands
SK Slovak Republic
SL Sierra Leone
SM San Marino
SN Senegal
SO Somalia
SR Suriname
ST Sao Tome and Principe
SU USSR (former)
SV El Salvador
SY Syria
SZ Swaziland

TC Turks and Caicos Islands
TD Chad
TF French Southern Territories
TG Togo
TH Thailand
TJ Tajikistan
TK Tokelau
TM Turkmenistan
TN Tunisia
TO Tonga
TP East Timor
TR Turkey
TT Trinidad and Tobago
TV Tuvalu
TW Taiwan
TZ Tanzania

UA Ukraine
UG Uganda
UK United Kingdom
UM US Minor Outlying Islands

US United States
UY Uruguay
UZ Uzbekistan

VA Vatican City State (Holy See)

VC Saint Vincent and the Grenadines
VE Venezuela
VG Virgin Islands (British)
VI Virgin Islands (U.S.)
VN Viet Nam
VU Vanuatu

WF Wallis and Futuna Islands
WS Samoa

YE Yemen
YT Mayotte
YU Yugoslavia

ZA South Africa
ZM Zambia
ZR Zaire
ZW Zimbabwe

COM Commercial
EDU US Educational
GOV US Government
INT International
MIL US Military
NET Network
ORG Non-Profit Organization
ARPA Old style Arpanet
NATO Nato field

Appendix B

Common spellchecker misses

While it is strongly advised to run the spellchecker when you have finished typing a word-processed document, it is equally important not to rely too heavily on it.

If you type too instead of to, for example, the spellchecker will miss your mistake. Similarly, if you confuse the different meaning of affect and effect, the spellchecker will not recognize your error, since both words are acceptable according to its criteria. Below is a list of some of the most commonly mis-typed, and commonly-confused words. Use a good dictionary to help you with any distinctions of meaning that are not clear to you :

a	ascent	began	but
an	assent	begun	butt
aboard	aural	bean	buy
abroad	oral	been	by
accept	axes	bellow	bye
except	axis	below	
addition	bare	berth	came
edition	bear	birth	come
advice	base	beside	can't
advise	bass	besides	cant
affect	be	bloc	cent
effect	bee	block	sent
affluent	beach	blond	cheap
effluent	beech	blonde	cheep
allude	bean	born	check
elude	been	borne	cheque
altar	bear	brake	cheep
alter	bare	break	cheap
alternately	became	bread	cheque
alternatively	become	bred	check
amend	bee	break	choose
emend	be	brake	chose
an	beech	breath	cite
a	beach	breathe	sight
angel	been	bred	site
angle	bean	bread	

110

clothes
cloths

coarse
course

come
came

complement
compliment

complemen-
tary
complimen-
tary

confidant
confidante
confident

conscience
conscientious
conscious

consul
council
counsel

continual
continuous

co-respon-
dent
correspon-
dent

corps
corpse

correspon-
dent
co-respon-
dent

councillor
counsellor

course
coarse

currant
current

dairy
diary

dependant
dependent

desert
dessert

device
devise

die
dye

died
dyed

discreet
discrete

discus
discuss

draft
draught

dual
duel

dully
duly

dyeing
dying

economic
economical

effect
affect

effluent
affluent

elicit
illicit

eligible
legible

elude
allude

emend
amend

emission
omission

ensure
insure

except
accept

excess
access

expansive
expensive

filed
filled

foregone
forgone

foreword
forward

forth
fourth

franc
frank

gaol
goal

gilt
guilt

goal
gaol

gorilla
guerrilla

halve
half

hanged
hung

hart
heart

hoard
horde

hole
whole

hoped
hopped

horde
hoard

hung
hanged

illegible
ineligible

illicit
elicit

immoral
amoral

impracticable
impractical

in
inn

inapt
inept

incredible
incredulous

inept
inapt

insure
ensure

it's
its

knew
new

laid
lay

lead
led

legible
eligible

licence
license

liqueur
liquor

loath
loathe

loose
lose

mat
matt

meter
metre

miner
minor

minister
minster

modal
model

moral
morale

net
nett

of
off

omission
emission

oral
aural

passed
past

personal
personnel

practicable
practical

practice
practise

principal

principle

program
programme

put
putt

quiet
quite

reign
rein

rap
wrap

read
red

ring
wring

risen
rose

rote
wrote

sail
sale

salon
saloon

scraped
scrapped

sent
cent

sloped
slopped

sociable
social

spared
sparred

speciality
specialty

stationary
stationery

steal
steel

storey
story

striped
stripped

summary
summery

super
supper

taped
tapped

their
there
they're

thorough
through

threw
through

tic
tick

to
too
two

ton
tonne

torturous
tortuous

vain
vein

want
wont

wave
waive

wet
whet

whole
hole

wont
want

wrap
rap

wrote
rote

your
you're

Index